Graceland's Table®

Recipes and Meal Memories Fit for the King of Rock and Roll®

ELLEN ROLFES

with

ELVIS PRESLEY ENTERPRISES

AN ELLEN ROLFES BOOK

Rutledge Hill Press®
Nashville, Tennessee
A Division of Thomas Nelson Publishers
www.ThomasNelson.com

Published by Rutledge Hill Press, a Division of Thomas Nelson Inc.,
P.O. Box 141000, Nashville, Tennessee, 37214.

Rutledge Hill Press books may be purchased in bulk
for educational, business, fundraising, or sales promotional use.
For information, please email SpecialMarkets@ThomasNelson.com.

Library of Congress Cataloging-in-Publication Data

Rolfes, Ellen, 1946-
    Graceland's table : recipes and meal memories fit for the king of rock and roll / Ellen Rolfes ; with Elvis Presley
Enterprises.
        p. cm.
    Includes index.
    ISBN 1-4016-0207-X (hardcover)
    1. Cookery, American. I. Elvis Presley Enterprises. II. Title.
TX715.R748 2005
641.5973—dc22   2005009607

Printed in the United States of America
05 06 07 08 09—5 4 3 2 1

TO GLADYS AND VERNON PRESLEY,

who instilled the values of the familial taproot in their son,

Elvis Aaron Presley,

including the meaning of the meal table

wherever it might be set.

Acknowledgments

Elvis Presley Enterprises, Inc., and Ellen Rolfes wish to thank the fans who contributed their personal recipes to be served at Graceland's table. Our special appreciation goes to those individuals who shared their favorite Elvis stories, which provide a glimpse into the indelible memories of his fandom.

For their unflappable commitment, we thank our agent, Liv Blumer, and our publisher, Pamela Clements. Countless thanks to Carol Boker and her meticulous recipe-testing/editing team; to Roy Finamore, our gifted food stylist; to Langdon Clay for his exquisite photography depicting variations of Graceland's table; to Susan Sherwood, the official Elvis photograpy assistant, who captured the photographic memorabilia.

Most of all, we thank Judith Kern, our talented text editor, who experienced an incredible journey as she wrote the interviews, and to Pete Davidson at EPE, whose steadfast devotion to the authenticity of the manuscript allowed us to present an intimate cookbook that takes the reader into other realms of the life of the King of Rock and Roll.

Contents

Foreword

As a train-riding, card-carrying, ever-loving son of the South, it is with deep conviction that I share this belief: Rock & roll music would not have the impact on the world as we know it had the Top Cat of Tupelo fueled his fire with tofu or sprouts. Elvis was a Southern boy. He was raised on Southern cooking and neither the U.S Army nor Hollywood, in all of its glory, could sway him off the course of his upbringing. He stayed true to the kind of food that put lighting in his step and caused the whole nation to shake, rattle and roll.

Who else but Elvis could make peanut butter and banana sandwiches famous around the world? Not a single journalist ever wasted ink on the fact that he could also has enjoyed a helping of grilled chicken or steamed broccoli from time to time. But the fact that he might have had a serving of bacon or two for breakfast at four in the afternoon seems to have caught the world's attention. Actually, it's really none of our business what he ate, or when. We should be mindful that a king's ways are not necessarily the ways of mere mortals.

Every aspect of Elvis's life was fascinating. He was like a diamond in that he sparkled at every turn. What made him shine the brightest to me was the music. His sound was a blend of all things Southern – rhythm and blues, gospel, the cry of a midnight train, cotton fields, honeysuckle, stealing a kiss from the prettiest girl in town, smelling mama's chicken frying as the sun goes down. His songs will forever drift through the universe like a beautiful dream. A dream that is sweet as the pie in this book.

—MARTY STUART

Introduction

It happened rather unexpectedly one Saturday morning—the day that Elvis Presley re-entered my life. My daughter and I were laboring to move a rickety, antique dresser with an attached mirror that I'd had since childhood from my attic to her new home. I noticed some yellowed fragments of Scotch tape left on the mirror by something I'd taped to it long ago, and in that moment I again "saw" Elvis staring back at me from those fragments. Instantly I remembered, as if it were yesterday, consciously deciding to put away my Terry Lee dolls forever in order to take a giant step toward becoming a "grown-up." At the age of thirteen I was still miserably torn between two worlds—playing with the dolls while simultaneously trying to relate to my more sophisticated friends who were already wearing bright red lipstick. I had long been ready to leave the little girl behind and begin the alluring journey into womanhood, but I'd needed a special someone to help me take that difficult first step.

I remember hearing my first Elvis songs on the transistor radio I'd been given for Christmas. Our whole family had gathered with dinner on TV trays to see him gyrating on Ed Sullivan's Sunday night television program. And, suddenly, I had feelings and yearnings I had never known. Like millions of others, I became obsessed with the weird surge of electricity that the sound of his mere voice created in my friends and me no matter where we were. With my allowance I bought 45 rpm recordings of "Love Me Tender," "Teddy Bear," and "Don't Be Cruel." That music was like a new language being sung to me by a wild, wonderful, beautiful man who had the courage to be like no one but himself, and it touched my heart. I think I fell in love.

I bought magazines with stories about Elvis and read them late into the night under the covers. I meticulously cut out and taped little black and white tabloid photos of him posed in every conceivable way onto my dresser mirror. My mother was horrified at my un-child-like behavior; but I, like countless budding teenage girls at the time, had found the musical icon who would escort me into another place. He spoke to me. He sang to me. I heard him. There was nothing anyone could do about it. Elvis was the man to walk with me over the threshold into adulthood, and my dresser mirror, before which I stood to look at myself each morning before school, became his shrine.

And so, on that day of laborious furniture moving, I smiled at those forgotten memories and began to tell my daughter the story behind the indelible tape markings that served as a permanent reminder of how Elvis Presley had shaped my life. Now I am a woman with mature responsibilities and grown daughters who have their own lives and loves, but that day I was a teenager again, revisiting my relationship with Elvis. I had not thought about him in a very long time, but as with any "first love," it took precious little to trigger instant memories and evoke long-forgotten feelings.

In all the years between, I have remained close to my Southern roots, and as I shared my memories with my daughter that day, I realized that Elvis, for all his fame and despite his public persona, had never left his either. At heart, Elvis was forever a country boy who had a deep connection to his Southern home and who craved simple meals with family and friends. He loved his mother's cooking—the comfort foods that nurtured and connected him to his familial taproot.

And so, as a cookbook developer, it seemed perfectly natural for me, in that moment of nostalgia, to imagine what it would have been like if I had been able to serve Elvis Presley a meal at Graceland's table, and then to wonder what other members of his fandom would have served the King of Rock and Roll.

Thus, communication with Elvis Presley Enterprises, Inc., soon followed, and we entered into a publishing partnership dedicated to capturing the collective imaginations of people just like me—those eternal fans who also would have given absolutely anything to have served such a meal or just to break bread with him. Together we went on a mission to honor the memory of Elvis Aaron Presley through some good cooking prepared as if for him. We put out the call for favorite recipes; we found obscure stories from well-known and not-so-well-known admirers; we searched the photographic archives for fan images; we even pretended to serve Graceland's table by staging exquisite food photography in his home—all for no other reason than to create a book written from the hearts of his fan base.

Now it is your turn. We ask you to partake of this fine food and fellowship and to imagine that Elvis Presley has re-entered your own life as you sit at your dinner table. Today, more than ever, we need such nurturing times together. And, like those markings on my mirror, Elvis will never be erased from our memories.

One

Appetizers, Party Foods, and Beverages

Graceland's Table

"Treat Me Nice" Chicken Salad

"Stuck on You" Burnt-Bacon Sandwiches

Peanut Butter and Banana Sandwiches

Jungle Room Party Sandwiches

"Let's Have a Party" Rye Bread Snacks

"Burning Love" Watermelon Salsa

Sausage Balls

"Are You Lonesome Tonight" Shrimp Wrapped in Bacon

Rock and Mexican Rollups

Sassy Southern Pimiento Cheese

"Just Pretend" Harvard Texas Caviar

"Spinout" Party Pinwheels

"Suspicious Minds" Clam Dip

"Double Trouble" Artichoke Spinach Dip

Pizza for Elvis

"Blue Hawaii" Waki Waki Punch

Almond Iced Tea

Frosty Sours

Tarragon Syrup

"Milk Cow Blues" Boogie Smoothie

"Stylin' Gent" Cocktail for Mr. Lansky

Quick Sangria

"Treat Me Nice" Chicken Salad

Yield: 26 appetizers

This is an appetizer for Priscilla.

12	ounces Italian-style chicken-breast strips, fully cooked
4	celery stalks, leaves included, finely diced
⅓	cup finely diced water chestnuts
⅓	to ½ cup diced toasted pecans
1	tablespoon finely diced fresh tarragon, or 1 teaspoon dried
4	tablespoons olive tapenade
1	teaspoon Dijon mustard
	Dash of fresh lemon juice
	Dollop of sour cream
	Dollop of mayonnaise
	Seasoned salt
	White pepper
26	endive leaves, washed and dried
½	cup cored, seeded, and coarsely diced yellow, green, and red bell peppers

➤ Combine the chicken, celery, water chestnuts, pecans, tarragon, tapenade, mustard, lemon juice, sour cream, mayonnaise, salt, and pepper to taste in a medium bowl. Chill, covered, for at least 1 hour.

➤ To serve, place the endive leaves on a serving tray, and, using an ice cream scoop, place chicken salad in each leaf. Decorate the tops of each with a scattering of the diced bell peppers.

VICTORIA C. STORM
Memphis, Tennessee

"Stuck on You" Burnt-Bacon Sandwiches

Yield: 10 to 12 sandwiches

I have been an Elvis fan my entire life. Through his life and music, he made me the person I am today. I think this recipe is very fitting, since all Elvis fans know how much he loved his burnt bacon.

1	pound bacon	½	cup finely chopped pecans
1	(16-ounce) jar mayonnaise	1	loaf white bread, crusts removed
1	(4.25-ounce) can pitted, drained, chopped black olives		

➤ Fry the bacon in a large skillet until very crisp (almost burnt); drain on paper towels.

➤ Crumble the bacon and mix it with the mayonnaise, olives, and pecans to form a spread.

➤ Spread a portion of the mixture on 1 slice of the bread and top with another slice to form a sandwich. Continue making sandwiches until the bread and filling are completely used up. Slice the sandwiches diagonally or into quarters to serve.

Cook's Note: This spread would also be good on toast points or crackers.

MARY ENGEL
Waxahachie, Texas

FROM ELVIS'S KITCHEN

Peanut Butter and Banana Sandwiches

Yield: 3 sandwiches

2	large ripe bananas	6	slices white bread
1	cup peanut butter	½	cup (1 stick) butter

- Peel and mash the bananas in a medium bowl. Combine the peanut butter with the bananas and mix well.

- Toast the bread lightly and spread the mixture on three of the slices; top with the remaining three slices.

- Melt the butter in a large skillet and slowly brown the sandwiches on both sides until golden brown.

Jungle Room Party Sandwiches

Yield: 20 to 25 sandwiches

½	loaf white bread, crusts removed	**FILLING 2**	
½	loaf whole wheat bread, crusts removed	1	(8-ounce) jar jelly or peanut butter
		1	(4-ounce) package dates or dried figs, chopped
FILLING 1			Lemon juice
1	(8-ounce) jar jelly or peanut butter		
8	slices bacon, crisply fried and drained		Chopped parsley and grapes, for garnish
2	Granny Smith apples, peeled, cored, and diced		
2	tablespoons heavy cream, or more or less as needed		

- Cut the bread into small triangles, squares, and circles. Mix the bread shapes so that you have one side white and one side whole wheat.

- Combine all the ingredients for filling 1 in one bowl and mix to form a spread.

- Combine all the ingredients for filling 2 in another bowl and mix to form a spread. Spread filling on a white side and cover with a whole wheat side.

- Continue making sandwiches, alternating the fillings, until all the bread is used. Arrange the sandwiches on a platter decorated with the chopped parsley and grapes.

MARGARET CRADDOCK
Memphis, Tennessee
Executive Director of MIFA, sponsor of Presley Place

Expanding Possibilities for Families

On a very hot July morning in 2004, in my role as executive director of the Metropolitan Interfaith Association (MIFA) of Memphis, I was proud to preside at the opening of Presley Place. Among its numerous charitable activities, MIFA operates Estival Communities, a group of more than 100 housing units for the homeless. Presley Place is our latest addition to Estival—twelve newly restored homeless housing units that were made possible by Elvis Presley Enterprises, Inc., through the proceeds from its auction of Elvis memorabilia held in Las Vegas on Columbus Day weekend 1999.

"In the fifty-eighth chapter of Isaiah, people of faith are challenged to share their bread with the hungry and satisfy the needs of the afflicted so that they could be called restorers of the streets on which they live. All of us in Memphis know that during his lifetime Elvis was very conscious of giving back a portion of what he'd been given to those who were in need, and EPE honors his memory by continuing that charitable tradition. During the time they spend living at Presley Place, families will participate in classes to improve their skills so that by the time they leave the program they will have become contributing members of the community. And so, through EPE, Elvis continues to expand possibilities for others."

MARGARET CRADDOCK,
Memphis, Tennessee

"Let's Have a Party" Rye Bread Snacks

Yield: 20 to 25 snacks

Elvis was all about food that wasn't fancy. This appetizer or snack is simple and tastes great.

6	**slices bacon**
1	**small red onion, chopped**
1	**cup shredded Cheddar cheese**
½	**cup mayonnaise**
20	**to 25 slices small party rye bread**

➤ Preheat the oven to 350 degrees.

➤ Fry the bacon in a large skillet until crisp. Drain on paper towels and crumble. Mix the bacon with the chopped onion in a medium bowl. Add the cheese and mayonnaise; mix well. Spread on the bread slices and arrange on a baking sheet. Bake for 5 to 7 minutes.

Cook's Note: Garnish with marinated artichokes or roasted red pepper if desired.

LISA MARTIUS
Lino Lakes, Minnesota

"Burning Love™" Watermelon Salsa

Yield: 8 cups

This salsa dares to be different. It's been a hit at every party where my mom has taken it.

6	**cups chopped watermelon**
1	**cup chopped green bell pepper**
¼	**cup chopped green onions**
¼	**to ⅓ cup chopped jalapeño pepper**
¼	**cup chopped fresh cilantro**
½	**cup lime juice**
2	**teaspoons garlic salt**
2	**to 4 teaspoons hot sauce**

➤ Combine the watermelon, bell pepper, green onions, jalapeño pepper, cilantro, lime juice, garlic salt, and hot sauce in a large bowl. Mix well and chill for at least 8 hours or overnight.

➤ Strain the salsa before serving. Serve cold with tortilla chips as a party food or as an accompaniment to grilled seafood.

KATIE GUBACHY, AGE 10
Livonia, Michigan
Official Elvis Insider

An Elvis Memory

I visited Graceland for the first time on Aug. 16, 2004—the anniversary day of Elvis's death and the 50th anniversary year of rock and roll.

Sausage Balls

Yield: 5 dozen

1	pound sharp Cheddar cheese, shredded
1	pound hot ground sausage or ½ pound hot and ½ pound mild
3	to 3½ cups baking mix (such as Bisquick)
2	tablespoons water

➤ Combine the cheese and sausage in a large bowl. Add the baking mix and the water and mix well. Roll 1 large spoonful of the mixture at a time into a ball. Place the sausage balls on a large tray, cover with aluminum foil, and freeze. Once the balls are slightly frozen, place them in a large sealable plastic bag.

➤ When ready to serve, preheat the oven to 350 degrees. Remove the sausage balls from the freezer and place them on a large baking sheet. Bake for 25 minutes. Serve hot.

SHIRLEY SADLER
Lebanon, Tennessee
TCB4EAP online fan club

Elvis never hesitated to take time to sign an autograph for a fan.

"Are You Lonesome Tonight" Shrimp Wrapped in Bacon

Yield: 6 to 8 servings

1	**pound medium shrimp**
1	**cup olive oil**
¼	**cup Cajun seasoning**
12	**to 14 bacon slices, cut in half**
	Chipotle barbecue sauce

➤ Combine the shrimp, olive oil, and seasoning in a medium bowl and marinate in the refrigerator for about 4 hours.

➤ Preheat the oven to 375 degrees.

➤ Wrap a half slice of bacon around each shrimp and secure it with a toothpick. Place the shrimp in a 9 x 13-inch baking pan and place it in the oven.

➤ Bake for 12 to 15 minutes or until the bacon is crisp. Brush with the barbecue sauce before serving.

KATY SUSTACEK
St. Louis Park, Minnesota

Did You Know?

In 1970 Elvis was chosen to receive the Ten Outstanding Young Men of the Nation Award given by the United States Junior Chamber of Commerce.

Rock and Mexican Rollups

Yield: 80 appetizers

These are a great change from regular tortilla chips dipped in salsa.

2	(8-ounce) packages cream cheese, softened
1	(8-ounce) container sour cream
1	(4-ounce) can chopped black olives, drained
4	green onions, both white and green parts chopped
12	ounces shredded Cheddar cheese
10	(10-inch) flour tortillas

➤ Combine the cream cheese, sour cream, olives, green onions, and cheese in a medium bowl. Spread the mixture over the tortillas. Roll them up and wrap foil around each rollup. Let them chill in the refrigerator for at least 1 hour.

➤ Remove the rolls from the refrigerator, remove the foil, and slice each roll into ¼-inch-thick slices. Serve with the salsa of your choice.

CATHY WAGGONER
Webb City, Missouri
Return to Sender Club

Sassy Southern Pimiento Cheese

Yield: 20 appetizer servings

This is an appetizer for Lisa Marie.

1	recipe "Roustabout" Cornbread (page 41) or cornbread mix
2	cups finely grated extra-sharp Cheddar cheese
1	cup finely grated Colby Jack cheese
1	(4-ounce) jar chopped pimientos
3	celery stalks, including leaves, finely diced
½	cup mayonnaise or salad dressing
1	tablespoon spicy brown mustard
1	teaspoon sugar, or to taste
4	to 8 dashes hot sauce
	Seasoned salt and pepper
	Pimento-stuffed green olives, sliced, for garnish

➤ Make the cornbread according to the recipe or package directions and set it aside to cool.

➤ While the cornbread bakes, combine in a medium bowl the cheeses, pimientos, celery, mayonnaise, mustard, sugar, hot sauce, and salt and pepper to taste. Cover and refrigerate until needed.

➤ Cut the cooled cornbread into 1½-inch rounds and place them on a decorative tray or a large serving plate. Using a small ice cream scoop, place some of the pimiento cheese mixture on each round. Decorate each with an olive slice and serve immediately.

Cook's Note: You may make the appetizers smaller, just bite-size, if you wish. Use a smaller scoop and make the cornbread rounds 1 inch each.

VICTORIA C. STORM
Memphis, Tennessee

"Just Pretend" Harvard Texas Caviar

Yield: 8 to 10 servings

1	(16-ounce) can black-eyed peas, drained and rinsed	2	tomatoes, chopped
1	(16-ounce) can black-eyed peas with jalapeños, drained and rinsed	1	(10¾-ounce) can tomato soup
		½	cup white vinegar
1	green bell pepper, cored, seeded, and chopped	¼	cup salad oil
			Dash of Worcestershire sauce
1	onion, chopped	1	cup sugar
2	avocados, chopped	1	teaspoon mustard

➤ Combine the peas, bell pepper, onion, avocados, and tomatoes in a medium bowl. Combine the soup, vinegar, oil, Worcestershire, sugar, and mustard in a second bowl and stir until the sugar dissolves.

➤ Pour the soup mixture over the vegetables. Refrigerate for 8 to 10 hours or overnight. Serve with tortilla chips.

Cook's Note: This keeps for about two weeks in the refrigerator.

JANE PERRY
Lufkin, Texas
Founding member, Official Elvis Insider

An Elvis Memory

My mother took my cousin and me to the movies to see Wild in the Country *because we were not allowed to go alone. When Elvis came on the screen, the whole place went crazy. My mother, bless her heart, asked, "Who's that?" My cousin and I could have gone through the floor. I don't think all the chaos was her cup of tea. After that, we could go to the movies alone. Thanks, Elvis.*

"Spinout" Party Pinwheels

Yield: 80 ½-inch pinwheels

Elvis loved people, cars, and good times. This recipe would fit his table.

2	**(8-ounce) packages cream cheese, softened**
1	**(0.9-ounce) package ranch-flavored salad dressing mix**
½	**cup minced red bell pepper**
½	**cup minced celery**
¼	**cup sliced green onion**
¼	**cup sliced green olives**
4	**(10-inch) flour tortillas**

➤ Beat the cream cheese and dressing mix in a medium bowl until smooth. Add the red bell pepper, celery, green onion, and olives; mix well. Spread about ¾ cup on each tortilla.

➤ Roll up tightly, wrap in plastic wrap, and refrigerate for at least 2 hours. Slice into ½-inch rounds before serving.

ELIZABETH E. KLAUS
Chattanooga, Tennessee
Founding member, Official Elvis Insider

Did You Know?

For many years Elvis donated at least $1,000 per year to each of fifty charities in the Memphis area.

"Suspicious Minds" Clam Dip

Yield: about 3 cups

Friends who claim not to like seafood will indeed have suspicious minds when they learn this tasty dip doesn't taste fishy at all. My mom gave me the recipe years ago, and it's been pleasing palates ever since.

2	(8-ounce) packages cream cheese, softened
2	(6.5-ounce) cans minced clams, drained, liquid reserved
1	small onion, finely minced
1	small fresh lemon, juiced
	Salt and pepper

➤ Put the softened cream cheese, clams, onion, and lemon juice in a medium bowl. Add a tablespoon or two of liquid from the clams to blend the cream cheese mixture. Add a dash or two of salt and pepper to taste and mix well.

➤ Refrigerate at least 4 hours before serving. Serve with butter crackers.

ELIZABETH ANDERSON
Mission Viejo, California

I Danced to Elvis's Music in My Crib

I have three older sisters, and they were big Elvis fans. My oldest sister, who is fifteen years older than I am, told me—because obviously I don't remember—that when she played 'Rock-a-Hula Baby' from the Blue Hawaii track, I would hold onto the bars of my crib and start dancing.

"The first thing I do remember is watching an Elvis movie with my sisters when I was maybe two, and that he seemed to me larger than life. He just stood out from everyone else in the movie. And as I got older I wanted to find out more about him. I was drawn to him; he had a presence that was different from anyone else I'd ever seen.

"I started to read books about him; and then in 1992, when I was seventeen, I actually lied to my parents and booked a Greyhound bus ticket to go to Graceland. It was the fifteenth anniversary of his death, and I wanted to go at a time that was significant, not just in any old year. I had the whole thing planned; I'd saved up a whole year for it, and I'd even booked my hotel room. When I first saw it, it was like going to Disneyland. Everything I'd read about and seen in books my whole life was right there in front of me. Sometimes it's hard to believe that someone like Elvis really existed, and Graceland just made it all real. It all came together. My dad found out where I'd gone and came to meet me there. He stayed with me for the second night before taking me home, and we got in line for the candlelight vigil. I remember standing in line with him, and when he realized how long the wait was going to be, even though he was a fan, he just said, 'You know, I didn't go through all this for my own parents when they died. I'll be at the hotel,' and he left. He said that to me in Italian, and when I told the people in line around me what he'd said, they all laughed.

"I'm a bigger fan than ever now, and I have a nice collection of things that came out while Elvis was alive—old movie magazines, buttons, books, concert tickets and memorabilia from the concerts, some of the Sun records, a lot of the albums, some sheet music, and a lot of posters—I like to get things that actually came out back then—collectibles from the '50s and '60s. We lived way uptown in Harlem when I was growing up. As a kid, maybe thirteen years old, I used to go downtown on the subway by myself to the record shops around Bleecker Street where they had the originals and buy a few records.

"When I was promotions supervisor for the Mets, we did an Elvis night at Shea Stadium. They were going to be playing at home on August 16, 2002, the twenty-fifth anniversary of his death. *Elvis: 30 #1 Hits* was coming out, and I thought it would be a great idea for a theme night. Since I work in marketing, whenever I have the opportunity and if it's appropriate, I try to do an Elvis event. So far they've all been hugely successful.

"When it comes to Elvis, I don't think anyone can look at him in a concert or in a movie and not realize that he had something no one else has. Even his face was unlike anyone else's. He had the voice and the moves, and even as a kid I could see that. Everything about him was unique."

STEFANO TROMBA,
New York, New York

"Double Trouble" Artichoke Spinach Dip

Yield: 8 to10 servings

From California to Memphis this would have been a great appetizer to serve in any of Elvis's homes.

1½	cups marinated artichokes with their liquid
2	(10-ounce) packages frozen chopped spinach, thawed
1	cup heavy cream
1½	to 2 cups grated mozzarella cheese
	Minced garlic or garlic salt
	Black pepper

➤ Preheat the oven to 350 degrees. Grease an 8 x 8-inch baking dish.

➤ Chop the artichokes into small pieces. In a medium bowl combine the artichokes with the spinach, cream, cheese, and garlic and pepper to taste . Spread the mixture in the prepared baking dish.

➤ Bake for about 30 minutes or until the cheese melts and the mixture is well heated.

CATHY WAGGONER
Webb City, Missouri
Return to Sender Club

Pizza for Elvis

Yield: 1 medium pizza

1	(4.38-ounce) package small-curd cottage cheese
1	large egg
2¾	tablespoons milk
2¾	tablespoons vegetable oil
½	teaspoon salt
1	cup plus 2 tablespoons all-purpose flour
1	tablespoon baking powder
1	(10¾-ounce) can tomato purée
	Cubed ham, pineapple chunks, sliced mushrooms, sliced pepperoni, sliced salami (optional)
8	ounces mozzarella cheese, sliced
	Oregano

➤ Combine the cottage cheese, egg, milk, oil, and salt in a large bowl. Combine 1 cup flour and the baking powder in a small bowl. Stir the flour mixture into the cheese mixture.

➤ Knead until you have a good dough, using the additional 2 tablespoons flour as needed. Roll the dough into a thin crust and place on a baking sheet lined with parchment paper.

➤ Preheat the oven to 350 degrees.

➤ Cover the crust with the tomato purée and add the optional items as desired. Cover with the mozzarella cheese and sprinkle with the oregano to taste.

➤ Bake for 15 to 20 minutes or until the edges are browned and the mozzarella is melted. Remove from the oven, cool slightly, and cut into slices.

ELVIRA KHAN
Oldenburg, Germany

"Blue Hawaii" Waki Waki Punch

Yield: 5 quarts (20 cups)

2   **quarts Hawaiian Punch**
1   **quart cherry soda**
1   **quart pineapple juice**
1   **quart lemon-lime soda**

➤ Combine the punch, cherry soda, pineapple juice, and lemon-lime soda in a large bowl and mix well.

➤ Chill for several hours. Pour over ice in a punch bowl to serve.

ELIZABET MCQUEEN
Parma, Ohio
Official Elvis Insider

Almond Iced Tea

Yield: 8 quarts (32 cups)

2   **tablespoons lemon-flavored instant iced-tea mix**
2   **cups hot water**
1½   **cups sugar**
2   **plus 8 cups water**
1   **(12-ounce) can frozen pineapple-orange-banana drink concentrate, thawed**
½   **teaspoon almond extract**

➤ Combine the tea mix and the hot water in a small bowl, stirring until the tea mix dissolves.

➤ Combine the sugar and 2 cups water in a Dutch oven. Bring to a boil and boil for 5 minutes.

➤ Stir in the tea mixture, the remaining 8 cups water, the frozen drink concentrate, and the almond extract. Chill. Serve over ice.

MARY RAINER
Lisman, Alabama

Frosty Sours

Yield: 2 cups

½	**cup bourbon**
1	**(6-ounce) can frozen lemonade concentrate**
1	**tablespoon frozen orange juice concentrate**
	Cracked ice

➤ Combine the bourbon, lemonade concentrate, and orange juice concentrate in the container of an electric blender; process until smooth.

➤ Gradually add the ice, processing until the mix reaches the desired consistency.

PATRICIA DEAN
Reston, Virginia

Tarragon Syrup

Yield: 2 cups

1½	**cups sugar**
10	**large sprigs fresh tarragon**
2½	**cups water**

➤ Combine the sugar, tarragon sprigs, and water in a heavy saucepan. Bring to a boil over medium-high heat. Boil about 1 minute or until the sugar has completely dissolved.

➤ Remove from the heat and cool to room temperature. Discard the tarragon.

Cook's Note: The syrup can be stored in the refrigerator for up to 1 month.

MARGARET CRADDOCK
Memphis, Tennessee
Executive Director of MIFA, sponsor of Presley Place

"Milk Cow Blues" Boogie Smoothie

Yield: 2 cups

This smoothie is made with TLC—just what a king needs when he's TCB (taking care of business).

2	**large ripe bananas**
2	**ounces chocolate banana smoothie mix**
10	**ounces cold milk or soymilk**
12	**ice cubes**
2½	**tablespoons peanut butter**

➤ Cut up the bananas and mash them in a blender. Add the smoothie mix and milk; mix well. Add the ice cubes.

➤ Blend until the ice is crushed and the mixture starts to thicken. Add the peanut butter and blend well.

Cook's Note: Place in the freezer for 1 hour for a great frozen smoothie.

CHARLOTTE CAMERON
Palmer Lake, Colorado
Elvis Weekly Fan Club

Elvis smiled at home cooking even away from home.

"Stylin' Gent" Cocktail
for Mr. Lansky

Yield: 1 serving

This recipe is named in honor of Guy and Bernard Lansky, from whom Elvis bought his clothes in Memphis in the early days.

	Fresh mint leaves
1	**teaspoon confectioners' sugar**
	Juice of ½ fresh lemon
	Juice of ¼ fresh orange
1½	**jiggers (4½ tablespoons) Jack Daniels straight whiskey**
	Crushed ice
	Cracked ice
	Dash of Triple Sec or other orange liqueur

➤ Muddle the fresh mint leaves and confectioners' sugar in the bottom of a chilled shaker. Add the juice from the lemon and orange and the whiskey.

➤ Shake thoroughly with the crushed ice and strain into a chilled cocktail glass or a bar glass filled with the cracked ice. Top with a dash of Triple Sec.

VICTORIA C. STORM
Memphis, Tennessee

Quick Sangria

Yield: 5 quarts (20 cups)

2   **(12-ounce) cans frozen pink lemonade concentrate, thawed**

1   **(33.8-ounce) bottle rosé, chilled**

1   **(33.8-ounce) bottle Burgundy, chilled**

    Juice of 2 limes

2   **(33.8-ounce) bottles club soda, chilled**

1   **lemon, thinly sliced**

1   **lime, thinly sliced**

1   **orange, thinly sliced**

➤ Combine the pink lemonade, rosé, Burgundy, and lime juice in a large bowl, mixing well. Slowly stir in the club soda.

➤ Garnish with the lemon, lime, and orange slices. Serve over ice.

BILLY GRESHAM
Sinking Fork, Kentucky

TWO

Breads
and
Breakfast Foods

Dill Bread

"Good Luck Charm" Overnight Buns

"Roustabout" Cornbread

Southern Cornbread

"For the Good Times" Eggnog Quick Bread

"Too Much Monkey Business" Bread

Dolly's Raisin Loaf

"Don't Be Cruel," Save-Some-for-Me Coffee Cake

Grandma's "Memories" Coffee Cake

"Promised Land" Breakfast Bread

Banana-Nut Bread

You Ain't Nothin' but a . . . Zucchini Bread

"Baby Let's Play House" Sausage Bread

"You Don't Have to Say You Love Me" Waffles

"Stuck on You" Caramel French Toast

"I Can't Stop Loving You" Egg Butter

"All Shook Up" Crustless Quiche

"Mystery Train" Eggs

Dill Bread

Yield: 1 loaf

This dill bread is as down-home, made-from-scratch, from-Mom's-kitchen as it gets.

1	**(0.25-ounce) package active dry yeast**
¼	**cup warm water**
1	**cup cottage cheese**
2	**tablespoons sugar**
1	**tablespoon dried minced onion**
1	**tablespoon butter**
2	**teaspoons dill seed**
¼	**teaspoon salt**
¼	**teaspoon baking soda**
1	**large egg**
2¼	**to 2½ cups all-purpose flour**
	Melted butter and salt, for topping

⯈ In a large bowl dissolve the yeast in the warm water. Heat the cottage cheese to lukewarm in a microwave oven and add to the yeast mixture. Add the sugar, onion, butter, dill seed, salt, baking soda, and egg; mix well. Add enough flour to form a workable dough. Cover and let rise 1 hour.

⯈ Preheat the oven to 350 degrees. Grease a loaf pan.

⯈ Punch down the dough. Place it in the prepared pan and let rise 30 to 40 minutes.

⯈ Bake 40 to 50 minutes. While still warm, brush with the melted butter and sprinkle with salt.

RACHEL KOPKE
Long Beach, California

"Good Luck Charm" Overnight Buns

Yield: 4 dozen buns

1	**(0.25-ounce) package active dry yeast**
1	**cup vegetable oil**
1	**cup sugar**
1	**tablespoon salt**
1	**large egg**
3½	**cups warm water**
4	**plus 4 plus 4 cups all-purpose flour**

Mix the yeast according to the package directions; let sit 10 minutes.

Combine the oil, sugar, salt, egg, and warm water in a large bowl. Add 4 cups flour and the yeast mixture. Add 4 more cups flour and knead the dough. Then add the remaining 4 cups flour and knead well. Cover the bowl with a clean cloth and let the dough stand 2 hours. Punch down and let stand for 1 additional hour.

Roll small balls of dough with your hands. Grease the cups of four 12-cup muffin tins. Place 3 balls of dough in each muffin cup, making a cloverleaf bun. Cover and let stand overnight.

Preheat the oven to 375 degrees and bake for about 15 minutes or until the buns have risen and are lightly browned. Serve hot or reheat before serving.

DELORES "DOLLY" JACKSON
Merritt, B.C., Canada
Merritt B.C. Elvis Fan Club

"Roustabout" Cornbread

Yield: 9 servings

Southern boys love to eat, and this cornbread would make them happy. Elvis probably would have loved it.

1	**cup all-purpose flour**
1	**cup cornmeal (yellow or white)**
2	**tablespoons sugar**
4	**teaspoons baking powder**
1	**teaspoon salt**
1	**cup milk**
¼	**cup oil or melted shortening**
1	**large egg, lightly beaten**

▷ Preheat the oven to 425 degrees. Grease an 8-inch or 9-inch baking pan.

▷ Combine the flour, cornmeal, sugar, baking powder, and salt in a medium bowl. Stir in the milk, oil, and egg, beating by hand just until smooth. Pour the batter into the prepared pan.

▷ Bake for 18 to 22 minutes or until a toothpick inserted in the center comes out clean.

Cook's Note: For bacon cornbread, fry 4 to 5 slices of bacon until crisp; drain on paper towels. Substitute bacon drippings for the oil. Sprinkle the batter with the crumbled bacon before baking.

LINDA CUNNINGHAM
Commerce, Texas

FROM ELVIS'S KITCHEN

Southern Cornbread

Yield: 6 to 8 servings

½	**cup vegetable shortening**
1½	**cups self-rising cornmeal**
1½	**cups self-rising flour**
1	**tablespoon sugar**
3	**large eggs**
2	**cups milk**

➤ Preheat the oven to 425 degrees.

➤ Put the shortening in a 9-inch, hot, iron skillet and place it in the oven until melted. Combine the cornmeal, flour, and sugar in a large bowl. Add the eggs and milk and stir until well mixed.

➤ Pour the mixture into the hot, greased skillet and bake for 20 minutes or until the top is golden brown.

Did You Know?

Elvis believed his movements were tame compared to dancing in the '70s and said that he "didn't do anything but just jiggle."

"For the Good Times" Eggnog Quick Bread

Yield: 1 loaf, about 10 servings

With the holidays being some of Elvis's favorite times, he would have loved this bread at the Graceland table.

2	**large eggs**
1	**cup sugar**
1	**cup eggnog**
½	**cup margarine**
2	**teaspoons rum extract**
1	**teaspoon vanilla extract**
2¼	**cups all-purpose flour**
2	**teaspoons baking powder**
½	**teaspoon salt**
¼	**teaspoon nutmeg**

➤ Preheat the oven to 350 degrees. Grease the bottom of a 9 x 5-inch loaf pan.

➤ Beat the eggs in a large bowl. Add the sugar, eggnog, margarine, rum extract, and vanilla extract; blend well. Add the flour, baking powder, salt, and nutmeg. Stir just until the dry ingredients are moistened. Pour into the prepared pan.

➤ Bake for 45 to 50 minutes or until a toothpick inserted in the center comes out clean. Cool in the pan 10 minutes; remove from the pan to cool completely.

Cook's Note: Add finely chopped pecans and/or white chocolate chips to the batter if you wish.

KAREN WHITE
Vancouver, Washington
Official Elvis Insider

Patty Parry: "They're Still Like My Brothers. . ."

We met driving down the street in Los Angeles. I pretended like I didn't know who he was, and he knew I knew who he was, and we just clicked.

"I was like a little sister to the guys, and they were totally protective of me. But I was also like a Jewish mother to them. We grew up together and they became my whole life. I remember when Elvis met my parents for the first time. 'Didn't I do a great job of raising Patricia?' he asked my mother. And she said, 'Yeah, I didn't have much to do with it.'

"I didn't go on tour with them because I still worked. I'm a hairdresser and I worked Wednesday through Saturday, and then I'd go wherever they were— Palm Springs, Vegas. . . .

"Mostly we just stayed in the hotel room and watched television. Sometimes the guys played football, but we couldn't really do very much. In Vegas we were like vampires; we slept all day and stayed up all night, almost never leaving our room. It's a very difficult life. Everybody wants it, but it's not the greatest life, especially with someone like Elvis. A lot of the rock and rollers today, the groups, they could walk down the street and no one would know who they were, but Elvis was very out there.

"So we sat in the room watching television, and mostly we ordered out pizza with lots of hot red pepper—enough to make us sweat. That's the way we liked it. The guys even put hot sauce on their watermelon. It's a Southern thing.

"Dinner was usually meatloaf and mashed potatoes. Elvis was a very simple eater. And for breakfast there was always loads of bacon. Whenever I smell bacon, I still think of Elvis. He'd have bacon and eggs with loads of salt and pepper on the bacon.

"In Memphis there was a cook, of course, and we had grits and red-eye gravy. He also had a cook here in LA for awhile, or Joe [Esposito] would sometimes cook. But in Palm Springs we mostly ordered in from pizza places, and we got bacon from Sambo's.

"I was a very lucky girl. But they were lucky to have me, too. I gave up my life. We were like a secret society; and now he's gone, and we were the only ones who shared his life. We still keep in contact, and I sometimes do fan club events with Jerry [Schilling]. The boys are sixty-eight years old now, but they'll always be my boys."

Patty Parry, Los Angeles
The only female member of the "Memphis Mafia"

Elvis and friends taking a break at Graceland.

"Too Much Monkey Business" Bread

Yield: 6 to 8 servings

This is a great breakfast or brunch item to serve for a large gathering, such as the group around the Graceland table on Christmas morning.

- ½ **cup chopped pecans**
- ½ **cup granulated sugar**
- 1 **teaspoon ground cinnamon**
- 3 **(10-ounce) cans refrigerated buttermilk biscuits**
- 1 **cup firmly packed brown sugar**
- ½ **cup margarine, softened**

➤ Preheat the oven to 350 degrees. Grease a 10-inch Bundt pan.

➤ Sprinkle the pecans evenly in the bottom of the prepared pan. Combine the granulated sugar and cinnamon in a small bowl. Cut the biscuits into quarters; roll each piece in the sugar and cinnamon mixture (or place the sugar and cinnamon in a zip-top bag and coat pieces that way). Layer the biscuit pieces in the pan.

➤ Combine the brown sugar and margarine in a small bowl; spread over the biscuits.

➤ Bake for 30 to 40 minutes. Remove from the oven, and cool in the pan for 10 minutes. Invert the biscuits onto a serving platter.

PAM DYSON
Ballwin, Missouri
Official Elvis Insider

Dolly's Raisin Loaf

Yield: 10 servings

A great quick bread for breakfast or after dinner, this is also an excellent offering for teas and other occasions of entertaining.

2	**cups raisins**
3	**cups cold water**
1	**tablespoon butter**
1	**cup sugar**
2	**large eggs, lightly beaten**
2	**cups sifted all-purpose flour**
½	**teaspoon salt**
1	**teaspoon ground cloves**
1	**teaspoon ground nutmeg**
1	**teaspoon ground cinnamon**
1	**teaspoon baking soda**

➤ Place the raisins in a medium saucepan. Add the water and bring to a boil. Boil for about 10 minutes or until the raisins are plump and 1 cup of water remains. If more than 1 cup remains, drain the excess from the pan before allowing the mixture to cool slightly.

➤ Preheat the oven to 375 degrees. Grease and lightly flour a medium loaf pan.

➤ Cream the butter and sugar in a large bowl. Add the beaten eggs and blend well. Sift the flour, salt, and spices together in a medium bowl. Add the baking soda to the raisins. Alternate adding the flour mixture and the raisins into the creamed mixture. When well blended, spoon into the prepared loaf pan.

➤ Bake for 1¼ hours or until a toothpick inserted in the center comes out clean. Cool completely on a wire rack before removing from the pan.

DELORES "DOLLY" JACKSON
Merritt, B.C., Canada
Merritt, B.C. Elvis Fan Club

"Don't Be Cruel™," Save-Some-for-Me Coffee Cake

Yield: 12 to15 servings

This is a simple, old-fashioned cake from a recipe I got from a neighbor in the early 1970s. It doesn't keep well because no one can resist having seconds—or thirds. Like Elvis, it has passed the test of time.

1	cup vegetable shortening
2	cups plus 4 tablespoons sugar
4	large eggs
1	teaspoon almond extract
3	cups all-purpose flour
3	teaspoons baking powder
¾	teaspoon salt
1	cup milk
4	teaspoons ground cinnamon

➤ Preheat the oven to 350 degrees. Lightly grease a 12-inch tube pan.

➤ Cream together the shortening and 2 cups sugar in a large bowl. Beat in the eggs and almond extract. Sift together the flour, baking powder, and salt in a medium bowl. Add the dry ingredients alternately with the milk to the egg mixture.

➤ Combine the remaining 4 tablespoons sugar and the cinnamon in a small bowl. Sprinkle some of the cinnamon mixture in the bottom of the prepared pan. Spoon one-third of the batter into the pan, and sprinkle one-third of the remaining cinnamon mixture on top. Continue by adding two more layers of batter and two more layers of cinnamon, ending with the cinnamon.

➤ Bake for 40 to 50 minutes or until a toothpick inserted in the center comes out clean. Cool right side up in the pan; then slide a knife around the edges and turn out, upside down, onto a serving plate.

SANDY STAEHLIN
Corvallis, Oregon
If I Can Dream Fan Club, Washington State

Grandma's "Memories" Coffee Cake

Yield: 6 to 8 servings

Elvis and I were from the same era, and he would have loved this cake, which Grandma fixed as a special morning treat for all of us to enjoy.

2½	**cups all-purpose flour**
1½	**cups sugar**
1	**stick (½ cup) butter or margarine, softened and cut in small pieces**
½	**teaspoon salt**
2	**teaspoons baking powder**
2	**large eggs**
1	**cup milk**
1	**teaspoon vanilla extract**
1	**cup raisins (optional)**
1½	**to 2 teaspoons ground cinnamon**

➤ Preheat the oven to 375 degrees. Grease and lightly flour an 8-inch round baking pan.

➤ Sift the flour and sugar together in a large bowl. Cut in the butter with a pastry blender or fork until well blended. Remove ¾ cup of the mixture and set it aside for the topping.

➤ Add the salt, baking powder, eggs, milk, and vanilla to the larger amount of flour mixture. Stir in the raisins, if using. Spoon the batter into the prepared baking pan. Combine the cinnamon with the reserved topping mixture. Sprinkle over the batter.

➤ Bake for 20 minutes. Serve warm.

GERRI MUCH
North Little Rock, Arkansas
Official Elvis Insider

"Promised Land" Breakfast Bread

Yield: 6 servings

The King would have graciously welcomed this bread at his Graceland table.

1	**loaf frozen white bread dough**
½	**pound hot sausage**
½	**pound bacon**
1	**cup grated mozzarella cheese**

➤ Defrost the bread according to package directions.

➤ Preheat the oven to 350 degrees. Grease a baking sheet.

➤ Crumble the sausage and fry it in a large skillet over medium-high heat until well browned; drain well. Chop the bacon into small pieces; fry them in the skillet until crisp and drain well. Roll the dough into an approximate 10 x 12-inch rectangle. Sprinkle the dough with the sausage, bacon, and the grated mozzarella cheese. Roll up the dough from one of the short ends and pinch the ends to seal. Lay the roll, seam side down, on the prepared baking sheet.

➤ Bake for 30 minutes. Serve with any style eggs.

NANCY MCMURTREY
Eden, Texas

An Elvis Memory

I was a young girl in the fifties and learned how to dance listening to Elvis's music. The magic in his voice has always lifted my spirits.

Banana-Nut Bread

Yield: 1 loaf

1	**cup sugar**
½	**cup (1 stick) butter**
	Pinch of salt
2	**cups all-purpose flour**
1	**teaspoon baking soda**
3	**ripe bananas, mashed**
2	**large eggs, well beaten**
1	**cup chopped nuts of your choice**

➤ Preheat the oven to 350 degrees. Grease and flour a 9 x 5 x 3-inch loaf pan.

➤ Cream the sugar and butter together in a large bowl. Sift together the salt, flour, and baking soda; add to the sugar mixture. Add the mashed bananas, beaten eggs, and nuts; mix well. Spoon the mixture into the prepared baking pan.

➤ Bake for 50 to 55 minutes or until a toothpick inserted in the center comes out clean. Serve with softened butter or cream cheese.

Cook's Note: For variation, add ½ cup chocolate chips and ½ cup peanut butter chips to the batter before baking.

JOHN DAWSON
Hurst, Texas
TCB Elvis Style Fan Club

You Ain't Nothin but a . . . Zucchini Bread

Yield: 2 loaves

3	large eggs
¾	cup vegetable oil
1	cup granulated sugar
⅔	cup packed light brown sugar
2	cups grated zucchini
2	teaspoons vanilla extract
3	cups all-purpose flour
4	teaspoons ground cinnamon
1½	teaspoons baking powder
1	teaspoon baking soda
1	teaspoon salt
1	cup chopped walnuts

➤ Preheat the oven to 325 degrees. Grease two loaf pans.

➤ Beat the eggs in a large bowl. Stir in the oil, sugars, zucchini, vanilla, flour, cinnamon, baking powder, baking soda, and salt; mix well. Stir in the walnuts.

➤ Divide the mixture equally between the two prepared pans. Bake for 1 hour or until a toothpick inserted in the center comes out clean.

ROSE MARY PULTZ
Tomahawk, Wisconsin

"Baby Let's Play House" Sausage Bread

Yield: 2 loaves

Elvis loved breakfast—especially burnt bacon and eggs. This sausage bread contains both bacon and eggs—a perfect breakfast for the King of Rock and Roll.

2	loaves frozen yeast-bread dough, thawed
2	pounds bulk sausage
1	pound bacon, chopped
1	bunch green onions, chopped
4	large eggs
1	cup freshly grated Parmesan cheese

➤ Divide the bread dough in half and allow it to rise according to the package directions.

➤ Brown the sausage, bacon, and green onions in a large skillet; drain. When cool, stir 1 egg at a time into the sausage mixture.

➤ Punch down both dough balls and roll each one into a rectangle. Spread half the sausage mixture down the center of each piece of dough and sprinkle the cheese on top. Bring the edges of the dough up over the filling and pinch along the length to seal. Pinch the top and bottom ends to seal. Transfer the loaves to greased cookie sheets and set them aside to rise again.

➤ Preheat the oven to 350 degrees. Bake for 15 minutes or until the loaves are golden brown.

MARY B. SETTLE
Assaria, Kansas
Founding member, Official Elvis Insider

"You Don't Have to Say You Love Me" Waffles

Yield: 12 (4-inch) waffles

1	**cup maple syrup**
3	**tablespoons chunky peanut butter**
3½	**cups baking mix (such as Bisquick)**
2	**cups water**
2	**large eggs**
½	**cup vegetable oil**
1	**cup chopped banana**

➤ Combine the syrup and peanut butter in a saucepan and place over medium heat until the peanut butter melts into the syrup. Keep warm while you make the waffles.

➤ Combine the baking mix, water, eggs, and vegetable oil in a large bowl, and stir with a wire whisk until smooth. Stir in the chopped banana with a spoon.

➤ Follow the waffle iron manufacturer's instructions to cook the waffles. Serve the syrup over the waffles.

MARY HANCOCK HINDS
Long Beach, California
Elvis on Capitol Hill Fan Club

"Stuck on You" Caramel French Toast

Yield: 12 to 14 slices

This would have been a great recipe to serve overnight guests at Graceland.

1	cup packed light brown sugar
6	tablespoons butter
½	cup cream or milk
1	teaspoon light corn syrup
3	large eggs
⅓	cup milk
½	teaspoon vanilla extract
1	loaf French bread, cut into 1-inch slices

➤ Combine the brown sugar, butter, cream, and corn syrup in a small saucepan and heat until smooth and bubbly. Pour into a 9 x 13-inch baking pan.

➤ Combine the eggs, milk, and vanilla in a shallow bowl; mix well. Dip the bread slices in the egg mixture and place in the baking pan with the caramel sauce. Cover and refrigerate overnight.

➤ Preheat the oven to 350 degrees and bake for 20 to 25 minutes. Serve immediately.

KATY SUSTACEK
St. Louis Park, Minnesota

"I Can't Stop Loving You" Egg Butter

Yield: 2 cups

This is a very old recipe from a black woman who lived with friends of mine years ago. Elvis would have loved it on his pancakes or angel food cake.

½	**cup (1 stick) butter**
1	**large egg, well beaten**
1½	**cups sugar**
3	**tablespoons light corn syrup**

¼	**cup water**
1	**tablespoon vanilla extract**
	Pancake or waffle mix of your choice

➤ Melt the butter in a small saucepan; cool. Stir in the egg, sugar, corn syrup, and water. Bring the mixture to a boil; cook for 1 minute.

➤ Remove from the heat and stir in the vanilla. Cover and set aside to cool while preparing pancakes or waffles according to package directions. Serve with the Egg Butter.

CHARLOTTE SMITH
Portland, Texas

Elvis enjoying a publicity photo with teddy bears.

"All Shook Up™" Crustless Quiche

Yield: 8 to 10 servings

This is no ordinary quiche. Made with bacon, broccoli, and pepper Jack cheese, it's a man-style quiche you can really sink your teeth into. Good enough for any man-size appetite and tasty enough even for a king.

½	cup crumbled crisp bacon
¾	to 1 pound pepper Jack cheese, shredded
12	large eggs, lightly beaten
2	tablespoons all-purpose flour, beaten with a splash of milk
1	(4-ounce) can sliced mushrooms, drained
2	(10-ounce) boxes frozen chopped broccoli, thawed and drained
1	cup sour cream (optional), for garnish

➤ Preheat the oven to 350 degrees. Grease a 12-inch pie plate or a 9 x 13-inch baking dish.

➤ Combine the bacon, cheese, eggs, flour, mushrooms, and broccoli in a large bowl. Pour the mixture into the prepared baking dish.

➤ Bake for about 45 minutes or until golden brown. Serve with the sour cream, if desired.

CHERYL WILSON
Bakersfield, California

An Elvis Memory

I saw Elvis in concert several times during the seventies when I was a teenager. One concert was in Long Beach, California. My aunt and my 10-year-old brother came to pick me up after the show. As they were walking from the car, they noticed a crowd gathering at the back of the building. They ran to check out the excitement. A limousine, dark windows rolled up, was exiting the building. People were gathering and screaming that Elvis was in the car. My little sandy-haired brother with his round freckled face grinned ear to ear as he waved at the closed window. Suddenly the car stopped, the window opened, and there was Elvis waving directly at my little brother. Then the window rolled back up and the car sped away. As I walked out of the auditorium, my little brother, eyes like saucers, excitedly told me the story of how he got to see Elvis.

"Mystery Train" Eggs

Yield: 4 to 6 servings

Here's a hearty and fulfilling breakfast entrée.

1	teaspoon butter
12	large eggs, beaten
3	tablespoons cottage cheese
½	pound ground sausage, cooked
2	tablespoons mild salsa
1	cup shredded Cheddar cheese

Melt the butter in a large skillet. Add the eggs, stirring until almost set. Stir in the cottage cheese and sausage. Add the salsa, stirring well.

Sprinkle the cheese on top. Cover the pan and let it sit until the cheese has melted.

JEANIE PUSSER
Las Vegas, Nevada
Viva Las Vegas Elvis Presley Fan Club

Did You Know?

Ed Sullivan paid Elvis $50,000 for three appearances on his show—more money than any performer had ever been paid for a network television variety show at the time.

Three

Salads

Graceland's Table

"Paradise Hawaiian Style" Brown Rice Salad

"Hard Headed Woman" Tropical Coleslaw

Mary's "Ready Teddy" Potato Salad

Corn Bread Salad

Mandarin Salad

Paradise Chicken Salad, Hawaiian Style

Tuna Seashell Pasta Salad

"And I Love You So" Super Salad

Vegetable Salad

Chopped Green Salad with Peanut Butter Dressing

"I Want You, I Need You, I Love You" Strawberry Pretzel Salad

"That Dream" Fruity Gelatin Salad

Moody Blueberry and Pineapple Salad

Tennessee Artichoke Pickle

"Guitar Man" Grape Salad

"Blue Christmas" Cranberry Salad

"Paradise Hawaiian Style" Brown Rice Salad

Yield: 8 to 10 servings

This light and tasty salad is full of fresh ingredients that would have delighted the King's taste buds and reminded him of a special place in his heart—Hawaii.

3	cups brown rice
5	strips smoked bacon, chopped
1	red bell pepper, chopped
1	ear of corn, cooked and kernels removed
1	cup unsalted peanuts
1	cup pine nuts
1	cup golden raisins
1	quarter pineapple, flesh chopped into small chunks
1	bunch green onions, chopped
5	tablespoons olive oil
3	tablespoons lemon juice
2	tablespoons soy sauce
1	garlic clove, chopped

➤ Cook the brown rice according to the package directions for about 30 minutes and spoon into a large bowl.

➤ Fry the bacon in a small skillet; drain. Add the bacon to the rice. Add the bell pepper, corn, peanuts, pine nuts, raisins, pineapple, and green onions; mix well.

➤ Combine the olive oil, lemon juice, soy sauce, and garlic in a small jar. Shake well, pour over the rice mixture, and stir to combine.

Cook's Note: If well covered, the salad keeps in the refrigerator for up to four days.

BARBARA SINGLETON
Patterson Lakes, Australia

"Hard Headed Woman" Tropical Coleslaw

Yield: 8 to10 servings

I created this dish with the tropics in mind. When I serve it, I never have any leftovers. The toasted coconut, trail mix, and pineapple bring coleslaw to new heights.

8	**cups shredded cabbage**
½	**cup shredded carrot**
¾	**cup chopped green onion**
1	**cup toasted, long-shredded, sweetened coconut**
1	**cup cranberry trail mix**
1	**(14-ounce) can pineapple tidbits, drained well**
½	**cup mayonnaise**
½	**cup sour cream**
¼	**cup heavy cream**
1	**teaspoon sugar**
½	**teaspoon onion powder**
¼	**teaspoon paprika**
	Pinch of pepper

➤ Combine the cabbage, carrot, green onion, coconut, trail mix, and pineapple in a large mixing bowl.

➤ Combine the mayonnaise, sour cream, heavy cream, sugar, onion powder, paprika, and pepper in a small bowl; whisk together. Add the dressing mixture to the cabbage; mix well.

➤ Refrigerate for at least 3 hours before serving.

GLENDA STAECEY
Colville, Washington

Mary's "Ready Teddy" Potato Salad

Yield: 8 to10 servings

The King deserves the best potato salad . . . and this is it.

10	**potatoes**
2	**pounds bacon**
1	**large onion, chopped**
1	**(34-ounce) jar salad dressing of your choice**
	Salt and pepper

➤ Place the potatoes in a large pot of water. Bring to a boil and cook until tender. Drain and cool. Peel and cut the potatoes into ½-inch pieces.

➤ Fry the bacon, drain, and break into small pieces. Combine the potatoes, bacon, onion, and salad dressing in a large bowl. Add salt and pepper to taste.

➤ Refrigerate until ready to serve.

MARY DANKS
Madison, Wisconsin
President, Elvis Connection Fan Club of Madison, Wisconsin

Corn Bread Salad

Yield: 8 to10 servings

12	sweet corn bread muffins
2	cups mayonnaise
1	large green bell pepper, cored, seeded, and chopped
1	medium onion, chopped
½	cup celery, chopped
2	tomatoes, diced
	Salt and pepper
4	to 5 pieces cooked bacon, crumbled

➤ Crumble the corn bread muffins finely in a large bowl. Add the mayonnaise, green pepper, onion, and celery; mix well. Stir in the tomatoes and season with salt and pepper to taste. Sprinkle the bacon on top.

➤ Refrigerate until ready to serve.

JOYCE CONRAD WILSON
Lexington, Kentucky

Did You Know?

Graceland was Elvis's home for twenty years. Today it is one of the most frequently visited homes in America with more than 600,000 visitors a year.

Mandarin Salad

Yield: 6 servings

1	**head romaine lettuce**
1	**(10-ounce) can mandarin oranges, drained**
1	**celery stalk, chopped**
1	**green onion, chopped**
	Handful of bean sprouts
¼	**cup canola oil**
¼	**cup distilled white vinegar**
2	**tablespoons dry mustard**

➤ Tear the lettuce into bite-size pieces and place them in a large bowl.

➤ Add the oranges, celery, green onion, and bean sprouts; mix well.

➤ Combine the oil, vinegar, and dry mustard in a small bowl; mix well. Pour the mixture over the salad greens, and toss lightly.

SHARRON ROWAN
Ontario, Canada

Elvis with Debra Paget on the set of *Love Me Tender.*

I Sat in Elvis's Big Pink Cadillac

When I was growing up, we lived in a little Delta town right outside Memphis called Robinsonville. That's where all the gambling casinos are now, but until then it was pretty much a ghost town.

"There was a drugstore there called Katz that had a huge revolving head of a cat outside; and inside, in cages, right in the middle of this general drugstore, there were exotic animals like little monkeys and snakes for sale. On this occasion, when I was about five or six, we pulled into the shopping center in front of the drugstore and there was Elvis's Cadillac parked outside. I think it was a 1955 model, but I'm not sure. "It was a convertible and the top was down and there was no one sitting in it. There was a bunch of guys standing around—his bodyguards or his friends, or whatever—but they weren't really hovering over the car.

"My sister and I were all dressed up like little ladies in our Sunday finest, which is how we always dressed to go to Memphis, and we just got in the back seat of that great big Cadillac and sat down. I remember that the rubber floor mats were monogrammed EP.

"We thought we were really doing it. We probably thought we were getting by with something, but chances are those guys were standing there watching us the whole time. Probably my grandmother knew they were watching us. And afterwards, I'm not sure people believed we really truly did it.

"We got excited about going to Memphis anyway, and going to Katz drugstore was like going to the zoo. Then to have Elvis's Cadillac there on top of it . . . it was almost like the Second Coming!

"I'm sure he was right there in the drugstore, but all I was thinking about was sitting in his car. To me that was a big deal. I wasn't even thinking beyond that to actually seeing him. It was awesome, and it's still a good memory."

SUE HODGE
Oxford, Mississippi

Paradise Chicken Salad, Hawaiian Style

Yield: 4 servings

This was a favorite of the late Julie Parrish, who costarred with Elvis in *Paradise Hawaiian Style*.

CITRUS DRESSING

1	(11-ounce) can mandarin oranges
½	cup mayonnaise
¼	cup sugar
1	teaspoon grated orange zest
¼	teaspoon grated fresh ginger
¼	teaspoon kosher salt
	Dash of white pepper
1	cup teriyaki sauce
1	cup pineapple juice

4	boneless, skinless chicken breasts
2	cups (8 ounces) iceberg lettuce
2	cups (8 ounces) mixed greens
2	(11-ounce) cans mandarin oranges, drained
1	pineapple, peeled, cored, and cut into chunks
1	mango, peeled and cut into chunks
½	cup (4 ounces) sliced almonds
½	cup (3 ounces) toasted shredded coconut
2	ounces rice noodles

➤ For the citrus dressing, blend the mandarin oranges, mayonnaise, sugar, orange zest, ginger, salt, and pepper in a food processor for 15 seconds. Adjust the seasonings to taste and chill until ready to use.

➤ Combine the teriyaki sauce and pineapple juice in a large bowl. Add the chicken breasts and marinate in the refrigerator for 4 to 6 hours. Remove the chicken from the marinade and discard the marinade. Grill the chicken for 5 minutes on each side or until tender.

➤ Combine the iceberg lettuce and mixed greens and divide among four chilled salad plates. Garnish the greens with the mandarin oranges, pineapple, mango, almonds, coconut, and rice noodles. Julienne the chicken and arrange it on top of the garnished greens. Drizzle each serving with the Citrus Dressing.

ROBERT ROSENCRANTZ, EXECUTIVE CHEF
Toledo, Ohio
Elvis Sweet Spirit Fan Club, vice-president

Tuna Seashell Pasta Salad

Yield: 8 to10 servings

2   cups small pasta shells, not cooked

2   (6½-ounce) cans tuna in spring water, drained and flaked

1   cup thinly sliced celery

1   cup thinly sliced green bell pepper

½   cup diced red onion

1   (4-ounce) jar pimientos

½   to 1 cup mayonnaise, as needed

2   tablespoons yellow mustard, or more to taste

2   tablespoons lemon juice

1   tablespoon distilled white vinegar

1   tablespoon dried parsley flakes

1   tablespoon horseradish

½   teaspoon celery seed

½   teaspoon dill weed

     Salt and pepper

     Paprika

➢ Cook the pasta according to the package directions. Drain and run under cold water; drain again.

➢ In a large bowl, combine the tuna with the pasta. Add the celery, green pepper, onion, and pimientos; toss to combine.

➢ In a small bowl combine ½ cup mayonnaise, 2 tablespoons mustard or more to taste, the lemon juice, vinegar, parsley, horseradish, celery seed, dill weed, and salt, pepper, and paprika to taste. Mix well. Taste and adjust the seasonings. Pour the dressing over the tuna mixture. If the salad is too dry, add more mayonnaise.

➢ Refrigerate several hours to blend the flavors. Serve cold or at room temperature in lettuce leaf cups or inside a scooped out tomato shell.

PAULA M. POST
Boca Raton, Florida

"And I Love You So" Super Salad

Yield: 8 to10 servings

This is a yummy salad that goes with everything.

1	large head cauliflower, cut into florets
1	large head broccoli, cut into florets
4	celery stalks, cut in ½-inch-long slices
1	(16-ounce) package frozen peas, thawed
1	pound bacon, cooked and chopped
¼	cup chopped onion
1½	cups mayonnaise
¼	cup sugar
¼	cup freshly grated Parmesan cheese
2	teaspoons distilled white vinegar
¼	teaspoon salt
	Black pepper
	Chunks of colby and Cheddar cheese, for garnish

➤ Combine the cauliflower, broccoli, celery, and peas in a large bowl.

➤ Combine the bacon, onion, mayonnaise, sugar, Parmesan cheese, vinegar, salt, and pepper to taste in a second bowl. Mix well, pour over the vegetables, and garnish with the chunks of cheese.

CATHY WAGGONER
Webb City, Missouri
Return to Sender Club

Vegetable Salad

Yield: 8 servings

Make this salad ahead of time for family reunions, church socials, or company dinners. This would have been a good salad for Graceland because there was always someone extra for meals.

1 **cup canned whole kernel corn**	1 **cup distilled white vinegar**
1 **cup canned small English peas**	1 **cup sugar**
1 **cup canned French-style green beans**	1 **teaspoon salt**
1 **(4-ounce) jar pimientos, drained**	½ **teaspoon black pepper**

➤ Combine the corn, peas, beans, and pimientos in a large bowl. Combine the vinegar, sugar, salt, and pepper in a small saucepan and bring to a boil, stirring constantly. Pour the vinegar mixture over the vegetables.

➤ Cool and refrigerate overnight or for up to one week.

JEANETTE THOMPSON
Hewitt, Texas
Memories of Elvis, Waco, Texas, fan club

Fan mania became a routine sight wherever he went.

Chopped Green Salad
with Peanut Butter Dressing

Yield: 4 servings

¼   **cup peanut butter, at room temperature**

1   **garlic clove, minced**

1   **teaspoon minced fresh ginger**

2   **tablespoons soy sauce**

2   **tablespoons rice wine vinegar**

1   **teaspoon sesame oil**

¼   **cup canola, vegetable, or peanut oil**
    Black pepper

4   **to 6 cups chopped hearts of romaine**

1   **tablespoon toasted sesame seeds**

➤ Combine the peanut butter, garlic, ginger, soy sauce, rice wine vinegar, and sesame oil in a small bowl. Whisk the ingredients to mix. Continue whisking while slowly pouring in the oil. Season with the pepper to taste.

➤ Divide the greens among four salad plates. Sprinkle with the sesame seeds, drizzle with the dressing, and serve immediately.

JOHN BOKER
Irvine, California

"I Want You, I Need You, I Love You" Strawberry Pretzel Salad

Yield: 10 to12 servings

This is a salad made with love and fit for a king.

1¼	**cups finely crushed pretzels**
½	**cup sugar**
½	**cup melted butter**
1	**(8-ounce) package cream cheese**
½	**cup confectioners' sugar**
1	**(16-ounce) container frozen whipped topping, thawed**
1	**(6-ounce) package strawberry gelatin**
2	**cups boiling water**
1	**(16-ounce) package frozen strawberries, with their liquid**
1	**cup drained crushed pineapple**

➤ Preheat the oven to 350 degrees.

➤ Combine the pretzels, sugar, and butter in a medium bowl; mix well. Press the mixture into a 9 x 13-inch baking pan. Bake for 10 minutes; set aside to cool.

➤ Combine the cream cheese, confectioners' sugar, and whipped topping in a medium bowl; blend well. Spread the mixture over the cooled crust.

➤ Combine the gelatin with the boiling water; cool. Add the strawberries and pineapple. Place the gelatin mixture in the refrigerator until partially set; then spread it over the whipped topping layer. Chill and serve.

DONNA STUTESMAN
Charlestown, Indiana
Elvis International Club

"That Dream" Fruity Gelatin Salad

Yield: 12 to14 servings

This recipe contains everything but the kitchen sink.
(In memory of my grandmother, Mildred E. Cox)

2	**(6-ounce) boxes gelatin, any flavor**
2	**ripe bananas, sliced**
1	**cup chopped apple**
1	**cup drained pineapple tidbits, juice reserved**
½	**cup sugar**
2	**tablespoons all-purpose flour**
2	**tablespoons butter**
1	**large egg, beaten**
1	**(8-ounce) container frozen whipped topping**
½	**cup chopped nuts**
	Lettuce leaves

➤ Prepare the gelatin according to the package directions. Stir in the bananas, apple, and pineapple. Place half the reserved juice from the pineapple in a small saucepan; add the sugar, flour, butter, and egg. Cook, stirring constantly, until thickened. Stir into the gelatin mixture. Pour into a 9 x 13-inch glass dish. Chill.

➤ Whip the whipped topping with the remaining pineapple juice. Spread over the chilled gelatin and top with the chopped nuts. Cut the gelatin and arrange the salad on the lettuce leaves.

LISA R. STEWART
Madison, Tennessee
Secretary, If I Can Dream Elvis Fan Club of Washington State

Moody Blueberry
and Pineapple Salad

Yield: 4 to 6 servings

This salad tastes great, plus the colors match the drapes at Graceland.

2	**(4-ounce) packages raspberry gelatin**
2	**cups boiling water**
1	**(8-ounce) can crushed pineapple, drained**
1	**(8-ounce) can blueberries, drained**
1	**(8-ounce) package cream cheese, softened**
1	**(8-ounce) carton sour cream**
½	**cup sugar**
1	**teaspoon vanilla extract**
½	**cup chopped pecans (optional)**

➤ Dissolve the gelatin in the boiling water. Add the crushed pineapple and blueberries and pour into a 9 x 13-inch baking dish. Allow the mixture to chill until firm.

➤ Combine the cream cheese, sour cream, sugar, and vanilla in a medium bowl and spread on top of the gelatin mixture. Top with the pecans, if desired.

MARGE HERRING
Lewisville, Texas

An Elvis Memory

I've been a fan since 1956. I've seen many concerts and visited Graceland often. The last time was for the fiftieth anniversary of rock and roll.

Tennessee Artichoke Pickle

Yield: 2 to 3 pints

Grandmother Luella Sterling served this each year as a Christmas relish with roast beef and Yorkshire pudding.

3	cups Jerusalem artichokes
1	onion, sliced
1	green bell pepper, cored, seeded, and chopped
1	red bell pepper, cored, seeded, and chopped
1	teaspoon mustard seeds
1	teaspoon salt
¼	teaspoon dry mustard
¼	teaspoon turmeric (optional)
¾	cup sugar
¾	cup distilled white vinegar

➤ Wash and slice the artichokes. Place the artichokes, onion, and peppers in a large pot with the mustard seeds, salt, dry mustard, turmeric, sugar, and vinegar. Bring to a boil, stirring occasionally.

➤ Place the mixture covered with the liquid in sterilized jars, or in a tightly covered container in the refrigerator for at least three days before serving.

SUSAN ROBINSON
Jersey City, New Jersey

It was a sweet, tender kiss

I'm writing a novel that's loosely based on my coming of age in Mississippi, and I want to make this story a part of that because it was so memorable for me. In 1970 Memphis didn't sell liquor by the drink. There were two clubs where people could bring their own bottle and be supplied with set-ups. I was twenty-one years old and working at one of them, waiting tables and trying to earn enough money to hitchhike through Europe. The doorman at the club had gone to high school with Elvis. One night he came up to me as I was finishing up my shift and told me that Elvis was coming to town and was having a party. He asked if I wanted to go—not with him, I should add, but by myself.

"When I was in second grade my mother had a crush on Elvis, and we went to see 'Love Me Tender'; everyone had cried. By this time I was into Bob Dylan and the Beatles, but I thought, 'oh well, this could be kind of interesting; why not?' I figured it would be a big party at Graceland, and I'd get to see Elvis only from afar. So the doorman wrote the address on a cocktail napkin, and I went home and changed into my purple fringed leather jacket and jumped in my car, which was a '55 Chevy my father had given me. It had come from Daytona Beach, and the salt water had completely rotted out the bottom. There was chicken wire where the floor had been. You could see the street through it, and the trunk didn't close all the way. It just kept popping up and down like a big jaw, and the tail lights had been improvised with red tape.

"By now it was about three o'clock in the morning. As I was driving along, I heard a siren behind me, so I pulled over and rolled down my window. The officer came up and said, 'You're out awful late, little lady.' I just looked at him and said, 'Oh, officer, I'm going to Elvis's party.' And with that he just sort of reared back and said, 'Well then, drive on.' So I did.

"At some point I realized the address I had wasn't for Graceland as I'd assumed, but it was for the local Ramada Inn. The guy from the club had written down the room number on the napkin. I knocked on the door, and it was opened by a young man with slicked-back hair and white buck shoes, who looked pretty much like the doorman who'd invited me.

"He stepped back without saying a word, and I walked in. And there was Elvis sitting on one of the twin beds next to a girl with a big beehive hairdo. There were a few other people in the room, but it was almost as if they weren't there. Elvis had on a chartreuse green shirt, a gold link belt, black pants, and black boots, and he was really strikingly handsome! I could feel a presence, an energy, a real animal magnetism. I went over and sat right down between him and the girl, and we started to talk. The more we talked the clearer it became to me that he was just a North Mississippi country boy, still naïve no matter where he'd been and what he'd done or how famous he was. I was flirting and carrying on, because he had that energy about him—he was Elvis.

"We talked and talked and finally at about five in the morning, I said I had to go. He stood up, and I really hadn't expected that. I thought, 'wow, he's a real gentleman,' and I remember being impressed that he had those manners. He asked if he could walk me to my car, and, of course, I said sure. So he walked me out of the room. We got to the car—which I was kind of proud of because I was into this reverse snobbery in those days—and I guess he was surprised because he said, 'Is this yours?'

"So, anyway, we were standing by the car, and he bent down and kissed me on the lips. It was a very sweet, tender kiss, and I remember being surprised by how sweet it was. There was a gentle tenderness about him that I just hadn't expected."

TRUDY DEAN HALE
Norwood, Virginia

"Guitar Man" Grape Salad

Yield: 12 to15 servings

This classic Southern dish is always a hit at family gatherings.

1	(8-ounce) package cream cheese, softened	2	pounds white seedless grapes, washed and dried
1	teaspoon vanilla extract	2	pounds red seedless grapes, washed and dried
1	(8-ounce) container sour cream		
1	(16-ounce) package confectioners' sugar	1	cup packed light brown sugar
		1	cup chopped pecans

➤ Combine the cream cheese, vanilla, sour cream, and confectioners' sugar in a large bowl. Fold in the grapes, and mix until well coated.

➤ Place in a glass bowl; top with the brown sugar and pecans and chill until ready to serve.

ANGELA JOHNSON
Muscle Shoals, Alabama

"Blue Christmas" Cranberry Salad

Yield: 8 servings

Befitting a Graceland Christmas

1	(6-ounce) package cherry gelatin	1	(8-ounce) can whole berry cranberry sauce
1	cup boiling water		
1	cup cold water	1	cup sour cream
		½	cup chopped pecans

➤ Dissolve the gelatin in the boiling water in a medium bowl. Add the cold water and mix in the cranberry sauce.

➤ Refrigerate the mixture until half set. Stir in the sour cream and pecans. Pour the mixture into an 8 x 8-inch glass dish and chill until firm.

MARGE HERRING
Lewisville, Texas

Four

Vegetables and Side Dishes

"Hunk of Burning Love" Green Chile and Cheese Casserole

"Love Me" Spaghetti Stir Fry

"Hound Dog" Hush Puppies

Swiss Green Bean Casserole

"In the Ghetto" Green Bean Casserole

"You'll Be Gone" Yummy Green Beans

"Jailhouse Rock" Baked Beans

"My Way" Broccoli Casserole

"That's All Right" Black-Eyed Peas

"Way on Down" Baked Corn

"Don't Be Cruel" Vegetable Hodgepodge

"All Shook Up" Baked Squash

Poke Salad Annie

"Burning Love" Executive Potatoes

Twice-Baked Potato Casserole

Home-Fried Potatoes

Hash-Brown Casserole

"Teddy Bear" Potatoes

Baked Sweet Potatoes with Raisins and Pineapple

"Hunk of Burning Love" Green Chile and Cheese Casserole

Yield: 8 servings

Smooth and rich with a touch of fire . . . that's Elvis's dance moves and this recipe. Both make you want to swoon.

¼	cup (½ stick) butter
1	cup chopped onions
4	cups cooked white rice
1	cup small-curd cottage cheese
2	cups sour cream
1	large bay leaf, crumbled or finely chopped
½	teaspoon salt
⅛	teaspoon pepper
1	(4-ounce) can chopped green chilies
2	cups grated sharp Cheddar cheese
	Chopped parsley, for garnish

➤ Preheat the oven to 375 degrees. Grease a 2-quart baking dish.

➤ Melt the butter in a small skillet over medium-high heat. Sauté the onions in the butter for 3 to 5 minutes or until tender. Spoon into a large bowl; add the rice, cottage cheese, sour cream, bay leaf, salt, and pepper.

➤ Layer half the rice mixture, then half the chilies, and then half the cheese in the prepared baking dish. Repeat the layers and bake, uncovered, 25 minutes. Garnish with the parsley and serve hot.

Cook's Note: Add browned, chopped chicken to the rice mixture before baking for a tasty main dish.

CINDY HUDSON
Juneau, Alaska

"Love Me" Spaghetti Stir Fry

Yield: 3 to 4 servings

Here's an easy, healthy meal to prepare for a king.

3	**tablespoons vegetable oil**
1	**small onion, chopped**
3	**mushrooms, chopped**
2	**medium carrots, sliced**
3	**ears baby sweet corn**
8	**snow peas or sugar snap peas**
6	**French green beans**
8	**small cauliflower florets**
8	**small broccoli florets**
⅓	**green bell pepper, cored, seeded, and finely chopped**
1	**cup vegetable stock**
	Salt and pepper
1	**(8-ounce) package egg noodles, cooked**
	Freshly grated Parmesan cheese

➤ Heat the vegetable oil in a large skillet over medium heat. Add the onion, mushrooms, carrots, corn, peas, beans, cauliflower, broccoli, and green pepper. Stir well and add the stock. Cover the pan and cook until the stock is almost completely reduced. Season with the salt and pepper to taste.

➤ Stir in the cooked noodles and toss well. Serve immediately, topped with the Parmesan cheese.

CHRISTINE RAYMOND
Ipswich, Suffolk, England

"Hound Dog™" Hush Puppies

Yield: 24 hush puppies

One of the first Elvis recordings I loved was "Hound Dog." This recipe would be wonderful for down-home, Memphis-style settings.

Vegetable oil for deep-frying
1   **large egg, lightly beaten**
1   **cup milk**
2   **tablespoons minced green onion**
1   **cup white cornmeal**
½   **cup all-purpose flour**
¾   **teaspoon baking powder**
¼   **teaspoon baking soda**
¼   **teaspoon salt**

➤ Heat the oil to 375 degrees.

➤ Combine the egg, milk, and green onion in a medium bowl. Combine the cornmeal, flour, baking powder, baking soda, and salt in a small bowl. Stir the cornmeal mixture into the egg mixture. Drop about 1½ tablespoons at a time into the hot oil.

➤ Cook for about 3 minutes or until brown. Drain the hush puppies on paper towels and serve warm with fried fish or seafood.

ELIZABETH E. KLAUS
Chattanooga, Tennessee
Founding member, Official Elvis Insider

Swiss Green Bean Casserole

Yield: 4 to 6 servings

A perfect side dish to serve with meatloaf or steak.

2	plus 2 tablespoons butter
2	tablespoons all-purpose flour
½	to 1 teaspoon salt
¼	teaspoon white pepper
2	to 3 teaspoons sugar
3	to 4 teaspoons grated onion
1	cup sour cream
2	(10-ounce) packages frozen green beans, cooked
1	to 2 cups shredded Swiss cheese
1	cup cornflakes, slightly crushed

Preheat the oven to 350 degrees. Grease a 9 x 9-inch baking pan.

Melt 2 tablespoons butter in a large saucepan; blend in the flour, ½ teaspoon salt, the white pepper, 2 teaspoons sugar, and 2 teaspoons onion. Taste and adjust the seasonings, adding more salt, sugar, and onion to taste. Stir in the sour cream and heat thoroughly; do not boil. Stir in the green beans and cheese. Turn the mixture into the prepared pan, top with the crushed cornflakes, and dot with the remaining 2 tablespoons butter.

Bake, uncovered, for 30 minutes or until bubbly.

CYNTHIA L. DENNIS
Hendersonville, Tennessee

"In the Ghetto"
Green Bean Casserole

Yield: 12 servings

Elvis was a Southern boy and he liked down-home cooking. He would have really gone for this dish.

3	**(16-ounce) cans French or cut green beans**
2	**(8-ounce) cans mushrooms, rinsed and finely chopped**
2	**cups chopped walnuts or pecans**
¼	**pound shredded Cheddar cheese**
1	**pound bacon, chopped, cooked, and drained**

➤ Preheat the oven to 375 degrees.

➤ Cook the green beans in a medium saucepan over low heat just until warm; drain and place in a baking dish. Stir in the mushrooms and nuts; mix well. Top with the shredded cheese.

➤ Cover and bake for 10 to 15 minutes or until the cheese melts. Remove the pan from the oven and sprinkle the bacon on top. Serve immediately.

Cook's Note: If you use fresh green beans, cook until crisp-tender before placing in the baking dish. This dish can be doubled or halved, depending on the crowd.

CHAR BLEDSOE
Lawndale, California
Official Elvis Insider

"You'll Be Gone" Yummy Green Beans

Yield: 8 servings

Elvis loved great Southern cooking. This is a different twist on an old favorite. Once these beans are on the table, they disappear.

2	**(16-ounce) cans cut green beans, drained**
½	**pound raw bacon, chopped**
½	**cup (1 stick) butter, melted**
½	**cup packed light brown sugar**
2	**tablespoons soy sauce**
	Dash of garlic salt

Place the beans in a large baking dish. Stir in the bacon. Combine the butter, brown sugar, soy sauce, and garlic salt in a small bowl; mix well. Pour the mixture over the beans and bacon; stir well.

Cover and refrigerate for at least 1 hour or overnight.

Preheat the oven to 350 degrees and bake the beans for 1 hour.

Cook's Note: Maple-flavored bacon adds a nice flavor to the beans.

CATHY WAGGONER
Webb City, Missouri
Return to Sender Fan Club

"Jailhouse Rock" Baked Beans

Yield: 6 servings

If the warden had thrown a party at the county jail, he would have served Jailhouse Rock Beans.

4	slices bacon, diced
1	small onion, chopped
1	(16-ounce) can pork and beans
1	tablespoon brown sugar
1	tablespoon distilled white vinegar
2	tablespoons ketchup

➤ Fry the bacon in a large skillet. When softened, add the onion and continue frying until the bacon is crisp and the onion is lightly browned.

➤ Drain the grease, leaving 1 to 2 teaspoons in the pan. Add the pork and beans, brown sugar, vinegar, and ketchup; stir well.

➤ Simmer, covered, for 30 minutes or bake in the oven at 300 degrees for 30 minutes.

DARLENE GUERRERO
Jasper, Indiana

Elvis on television changed the
American culture forever.

"My Way"
Broccoli Casserole

Yield: 6 servings

Elvis went through life doing things his way, but he never forgot where he came from or his family and friends.

2	(10-ounce) packages frozen cut broccoli, thawed
¾	pound sliced Velveeta cheese
½	cup (1 stick) butter or margarine
15	saltine crackers, crushed

Cook the broccoli according to the package directions; drain and place in a 3-quart casserole dish.

Preheat the oven to 375 degrees.

Place the cheese slices over the broccoli. Melt the butter in a medium saucepan over low heat. Stir the crackers into the melted butter, coating them well. Spread the crackers over the cheese.

Bake, uncovered, 20 minutes or until the cheese bubbles and the crackers brown lightly.

SANDY WAREHIME
Amarillo, Texas
Elvis Friends Are the Best, president

"That's All Right" Black-Eyed Peas

Yield: 10 servings

Elvis would smack his lips over this recipe.

1	pound smoked sausage, sliced
2	medium onions, chopped
1	medium green bell pepper, cored, seeded, and chopped
4	cloves garlic, minced
1	(8-ounce) can tomato sauce
3	(15½-ounce) cans shelled black-eyed peas
1	ham-flavored bouillon cube
½	to 1 teaspoon ground red pepper
1	teaspoon black pepper
1	cup chopped fresh parsley

➤ Brown the sausage in a Dutch oven over medium heat, stirring occasionally. Remove from the pan and drain.

➤ Sauté the onions, bell pepper, and garlic in the Dutch oven until tender. Stir in the sausage, tomato sauce, black-eyed peas, bouillon cube, red pepper, and black pepper. Cook until thoroughly heated, stirring often. Stir in the parsley just before serving.

CINDY BROWN BROOKS
Greenville, Texas

"Way on Down" Baked Corn

Yield: 8 to 10 servings

Anyone who enjoys down-home recipes will savor this dish.

½	**box (2 sleeves) saltine crackers, crushed**
4	**(16-ounce) cans cream-style corn**
2	**tablespoons milk**
	Pats of butter

- Preheat the oven to 350 degrees. Grease a 9 x 13-inch baking pan.

- Crush the crackers. Layer the cracker crumbs and corn alternately in the prepared pan, ending with a layer of crumbs. Make a well in the center and add the milk. Place the pats of butter about 3 to 4 inches apart on top of the crumbs.

- Bake for 45 minutes or until well browned on top. Serve with fried chicken.

JAN FRANSEN
Bellingham, Washington

Did You Know?

Elvis was in the first group ever to be inducted into the Rock and Roll Hall of Fame in 1986.

"Don't Be Cruel" Vegetable Hodgepodge

Yield: 4 to 6 servings

I think Elvis would have liked this because he was a lover of good home cooking.

1	**pound baby carrots, peeled and chopped**
1	**pound green beans, ends removed, beans cut in half**
1	**pound yellow beans, ends removed, beans cut in half**
2	**pounds small new potatoes with skin on**
1	**quart (4 cups) cream**
¼	**pound (1 stick) butter**
	Salt and pepper

➢ Place the carrots, beans, and potatoes in a large heavy pot. Cover with water and cook over medium heat until crisp-tender. Drain the vegetables and return them to the pot. Add the cream and butter; stir well.

➢ Simmer for 30 to 45 minutes or until the vegetables are tender. Season with salt and pepper to taste.

➢ Serve with fried, Cajun-style pork chops.

LEONA L. MOLBURY
Nova Scotia, Canada

A Great Performer and a Great Person

I grew up in Chicago—on Mayor Daley's block, for that matter—and my first recollection of being interested in Elvis is when I was about ten years old and *Roustabout* came out. After I saw a few more of Elvis's movies, if there was anything about him on the news or a story in one of the papers, I was always eager to hear or read it. There was always something mystical about him that intrigued me, but it wasn't until after he died that my interest was really piqued to find out more of what he was about.

"I made my first trip to Memphis in '83, and, of course, I took the tour of Graceland. I remember thinking it was very impressive. From the outside it looked quite massive and grand. But when I went inside I was surprised to see how small the rooms are. Since it was built in 1939, though, the rooms were probably quite large for that time. I guess I'd just expected it to be somehow larger than life. I remember feeling comfortable there, and I thought it really fit Elvis.

"I went back to Graceland in 1996. That's when I really wanted to find out more. I wondered what Elvis used to do in that town when he wasn't working, before he went to school, and before he became famous. I went to Sun Studios and that started me on my own project. For the last several years I've been working on a travel guide of Memphis and Tupelo that so far includes more than two hundred Elvis-related sites in Memphis and about fifty in Tupelo. I also do research on the sites to include any historical value they might have. Some of the sites have been lost to the wrecking ball, but a lot of them—including four of his homes—are still standing. In fact, they've just renovated and reopened Lauderdale Courts, the Memphis federal housing project in which he lived. They've reconditioned the

Presleys' apartment to look the way it did when he was there, and you can now take a tour of Elvis's apartment.

"There was also an auction in 1996 held by Butterfield & Butterfield in San Francisco. I bought a ring Elvis had owned and a TCB—taking care of business—necklace he'd given to Jackie Kahane, the comedian who opened for him in Vegas. He gave those to the guys to signify he thought they were 'okay.' If you got one, you knew you were part of the group. He gave the girls TLC necklaces—for tender loving care. I also bought a pair of his sunglasses and two of his bedroom lamps. That was the beginning of my collecting, and by now I've got quite a large collection.

"Since then I've been going back to Graceland twice a year—for his birthday and for Elvis week. I just think Elvis was cool without even knowing it. I like where he came from and where he went. Everything about him intrigues me—his connection to his father and the fact that he was so charitable because he knew what it was to want. And I don't think anybody would argue with the fact that he had a voice like nobody else. People keep trying to copy it, but nobody has. He was just a great performer and a great person."

BILL CALES
Chicago, Illinois

The "King of Rock & Roll."

"All Shook Up" Baked Squash

Yield: 6 servings

No Southern table, including Graceland's, would be complete without a sweet vegetable.

4	**slices bacon, chopped**
1	**small onion, chopped**
1	**(16-ounce) can yellow squash, drained, or 4 to 6 small yellow squash, sliced and cooked**
½	**cup evaporated milk**
¼	**cup packed light brown sugar**
2	**large eggs**
	Salt and pepper
1	**sleeve saltine crackers, crushed**

▶ Preheat the oven to 350 degrees.

▶ Sauté the bacon and the onion in a small skillet. Spoon the squash into a medium bowl. Add the bacon and onion. Stir in the milk, brown sugar, eggs, and salt and pepper to taste; mix well. Thicken the mixture slightly with a small portion of the crushed saltine crackers. Pour into a 2½-quart casserole dish and top with the remaining crackers.

▶ Bake 30 minutes or until brown on top.

JANE PERRY
Lufkin, Texas
Founding member, Official Elvis Insider

Poke Salad Annie

Yield: 4 servings

Serve this dish with fresh buttered cornbread on the side and you have a meal fit for the king.

2	**pounds freshly picked, young poke salad leaves**
½	**pound thick-sliced bacon**
1	**medium onion, chopped**
	Hot sauce
	Hard-cooked egg (optional)

➤ Wash the poke leaves. Parboil the leaves and stems twice in a medium saucepan, pouring off the water each time after parboiling (about 15 minutes). Boil a third time in clean water for 20 to 30 minutes or until tender. Rinse and drain well.

➤ Fry the bacon and remove from the pan. Add the onion and the greens and cook in the bacon drippings about 15 to 20 minutes or until tender. Add the hot sauce to taste, and serve topped with the bacon and a sliced hard-cooked egg, if desired.

Cook's Note: Pokeweed, which grows throughout the South, provides tender spring greens. If you can't find poke salad, use any other greens, such as kale, turnip, or collard. If using milder-flavored greens, clean them well and go directly to the sautéing stage. A salad spinner helps to get the greens clean.

ANNE FARRELL
St. Petersburg Beach, Florida

"Burning Love" Executive Potatoes

Yield: 8 to 10 servings

This spiced-up version of mashed potatoes would complement any meat served at Graceland.

6	medium baking potatoes
4	plus 2 tablespoons butter
3	cups sour cream
⅓	cup chopped green onions
2	plus ½ cups grated Cheddar cheese
1	teaspoon salt
¼	teaspoon pepper

➤ Boil the potatoes until tender. Cool, then peel the cooked potatoes.

➤ Preheat the oven to 350 degrees. Grease a 9 x 13-inch baking dish.

➤ Grate the potatoes into a large bowl. Mix in 4 tablespoons butter, the sour cream, green onions, 2 cups grated cheese, and the salt and pepper. Spoon the potato mixture into the prepared baking dish. Dot with the remaining 2 tablespoons of butter and bake, uncovered, for 35 to 40 minutes. Remove from the oven and top with the remaining ½ cup cheese.

Cook's Note: You can freeze the potatoes in their pan before baking. When ready to use, thaw and then bake as recommended. Cover with foil the first 15 minutes of baking time.

KAREN WHITE
Vancouver, Washington
Official Elvis Insider

"Just Pretend" Harvard Texas Caviar (page 25) with stacked Saltines is ready for guests entering the Music Room.

(TOP)
A family portrait photo of young Elvis with his parents, Gladys and Vernon Presley, captures his strong familial roots.

(BOTTOM)
Minnie Mae Presley serves a modest meal at the kitchen table to her son Vernon and grandson Elvis.

(TOP)
The Jungle Room with its thematic décor is designed for casual entertainment.

(BOTTOM)
"King Creole" Shrimp Creole (page 172) awaits the Elvis entourage by the fountain in the Jungle Room.

A *Graceland's Table*
EXCLUSIVE
Photo by Langdon Clay

(TOP)
"Taking Care of Business" Meat Loaf (page 116) with "In the Ghetto" Green Bean Casserole (page 85) are served buffet style on the stove in Graceland's kitchen.

(BOTTOM)
Graceland's spacious kitchen was used 24/7 with a round-the-clock cook always on standby.

A *Graceland's Table* **EXCLUSIVE**
Photo by Langdon Clay

The budding teenage girls were at the heart of the Elvis fan base.

Elvis poses with the Maid of Cotton to promote a charity event in Memphis.

(TOP)
The living room at Grace-land is timeless in its serene white and sky blue décor.

(BOTTOM)
The music room houses the handsome baby grand piano.

Paradise Chicken Salad, Hawaiian Style (page 67) is an inviting summer entrée set beside the photo of Elvis's parents.

(TOP)
His smile alone makes a memory for a lifetime.

(BOTTOM)
Elvis was the most at home at Graceland.

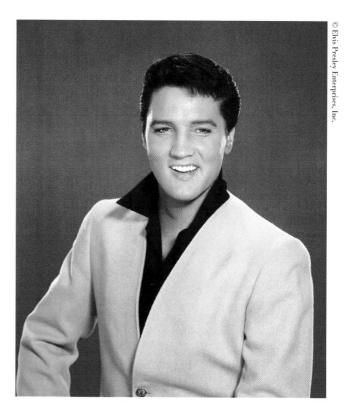

(TOP)
*"It's Easy for You" Coconut Chicken
(page 147) with Vegetable Salad (page 70)
is an elegant meal for guests served at
Graceland's table.*

(BOTTOM)
*The wildlife figurines draw
attention on the exotic table
in the Jungle Room.*

*A serving dish of "All Shook Up™"
Hound Dogs (page 117) waits to fill
up guests in the TV Room.*

(TOP)
The Elvis 45 record collection housed all types of music ready to play for an "all nighter" at Graceland.

(BOTTOM)
The formal dining room at Graceland was frequently used by Elvis for dinner with family and friends.

(TOP)
The musical gates of Graceland welcome everyone.

(BOTTOM)
A "Fever" Sandwich (page 105) is the perfect lunch break at Vernon's office desk.

"Can't Help Falling in Love" with Southern Pecan Pie (page 200) makes guests stop from a game in the Pool Room.

(TOP)

*Scatter Chunky Monkey Parfaits
(page 205) complement the monkey
motif in the TV Room.*

(TOP)
The elaborate TV Room is an unforgettable setting where Elvis entertained his close circle of friends.

(BOTTOM)
"Too Much Money Business" Bread (page 46) is cleverly served beside the posing monkey in the TV Room.

Elvis loved to sign autographs
with his adoring fans.

There is none other
like the King of
Rock & Roll®

Twice-Baked Potato Casserole

Yield: 6 to 8 servings

6	to 8 small to medium potatoes
1	(16-ounce) container sour cream
1	tablespoon garlic powder with parsley
¼	cup (4 tablespoons) butter
1	(8-ounce) package sharp Cheddar cheese, shredded, divided
¼	to ⅓ cup milk

➤ Bake or microwave the potatoes until they are soft but not mushy; set aside to cool. Preheat the oven to 350 degrees.

➤ Dice the potatoes and place them in a large bowl. Add the sour cream, garlic powder, butter, and half the cheese. Mix well, adding milk as needed to produce a mixture of batter consistency. Spoon the mixture into a 9 x 13-inch baking dish and top with the remaining cheese.

➤ Bake for 25 minutes or until the cheese is melted and lightly browned.

Cook's Note: Add finely chopped, sautéed onions to the potato mixture, if desired.

JOANN W. BUIE
Bogue Chitto, Mississippi

Elvis created a persona of a "ladies' man."

FROM ELVIS'S KITCHEN

Home-Fried Potatoes

Yield: 4 to 6 servings

1½	tablespoons vegetable shortening
4	large potatoes, peeled and sliced
2	onions, sliced
1	teaspoon salt
1	teaspoon pepper

➤ Heat the shortening in a large skillet. Add the potatoes and fry slowly for about 25 minutes, turning frequently.

➤ Add the onions, salt, and pepper. Continue cooking for an additional 15 minutes.

Hash-Brown Casserole

Yield: 6 to 8 servings

1	(1-pound, 10-ounce) package frozen hash browns, thawed	1	small onion, finely chopped
2	(10¾-ounce) cans cream of chicken soup	1	pound shredded Cheddar cheese Salt and pepper

➤ Preheat the oven to 350 degrees. Lightly grease a 9 x 13-inch baking pan.

➤ Combine the hash browns, soup, onion, and cheese in a large bowl; mix well. Add the salt and pepper to taste. Bake for 30 or 40 minutes or until golden brown.

SHARON PARKER
LaVergne, Tennessee
Official Elvis Insider

"Teddy Bear™" Potatoes

Yield: 6 servings

This is a quick and filling side dish.

5	**medium potatoes, washed and sliced, with skins**
1	**small onion, chopped**
1	**celery stalk, sliced**
½	**cup water**
1	**tablespoon butter or margarine**
1	**teaspoon chopped garlic**
½	**teaspoon celery seed**
½	**teaspoon dried basil**
1	**teaspoon dried parsley**
	Salt and pepper

➤ Layer the potatoes, onion, and celery in a microwave-safe casserole dish. Add the water and dot with the butter. Combine the garlic, celery seed, basil, parsley, and salt and pepper to taste and season the potatoes.

➤ Cook, covered, on high in the microwave for 3 minutes or until the butter melts. Stir to mix all the ingredients. Microwave, covered, on high for 15 minutes or until the potatoes are tender. Remove and serve immediately.

Cook's Note: You can add chopped mushrooms to the potato mixture or sprinkle shredded Cheddar cheese over the potatoes before serving.

GINGER LENNON
Euclid, Ohio
Elvis Shake, Rattle & Roll Fan Club president

Baked Sweet Potatoes with Raisins and Pineapple

Yield: 8 servings

I was born the year Elvis starting recording, 1954. Every time I eat good food, I think Elvis is watching me.

1¾	pounds unpeeled sweet potatoes (about 4 small potatoes)	¼	teaspoon ground cinnamon
½	cup raisins	1	(8-ounce) can unsweetened crushed pineapple, drained
2	tablespoons light brown sugar	2	tablespoons chopped pecans

➤ Wash the sweet potatoes. Microwave on high for about 15 minutes or until fork tender. Let cool 15 minutes, then peel and place the potatoes in a medium bowl.

➤ Preheat the oven to 400 degrees.

➤ Mash the potatoes. Stir in the raisins, brown sugar, cinnamon, and pineapple; mix well. Spoon the mixture into a 9-inch pie pan and sprinkle with the chopped pecans. Bake for 15 minutes.

Cook's Note: If you do not have a microwave oven, bake the potatoes at 400 degrees for 1 hour or until done.

EVELYN J. SMART
Pawleys Island, South Carolina
Official Elvis Insider

Five

Meats

Don't Drip on My "Blue Suede Shoes" Steak in Redeye Gravy

"Don't Cry Daddy" Round Steak Sauerbraten

"Fever" Sandwiches

"My Way" Cottage Pie

"Burning Love" Tater Tot Casserole

Memories Meat Loaf

"Surrender" Best Ever Buttermilk Meat Loaf

"Promised Land" Hash

"Stay Away" Sloppy Joes

Cheeseburger

"Never Been to Spain" Spanish Delight

"Taking Care of Business" Meat Loaf

"All Shook Up" Hound Dogs

"Trying to Get to You" Porcupine Meatballs

"Viva Las Vegas" Pasta Dish

Memphis Veal on a Stick

"One Night" Hamburger and Potato Casserole

"Coney Island" Hot Dogs with Hound Sauce

"I'm a Roustabout" Chuck Roast

Viva La-S'getti

"Change of Habit" Spaghetti Cake

"G.I. Blues" Brown Beef Gravy

"Burning Love" Pepper Steak

"The Lady Loves Me" Sunday Baked Ham

"Mean Woman Blues" Ribs

Special Barbecue Sauce

"If I Could Dream" Zucchini Casserole

"Rock-a-Hula" Ham

"Blue Hawaii" Sweet and Sour Hawaiian Spareribs

"Stuck on You" Sausage Scaloppini

"Big Boss Man" Italian Sausage Bombers

Don't Drip on My "Blue Suede Shoes™" Steak in Redeye Gravy

Yield: 4 to 6 servings

Elvis and his buddies would have loved this versatile, inexpensive, and delicious steak with down-home flavor.

1	(10¾-ounce) can tomato soup
1	(8-ounce) can mushroom steak sauce
3	to 4 tablespoons ketchup
1	to 2 teaspoons mustard
1	teaspoon Worcestershire sauce
	Sugar
1	to 2 cups all-purpose flour
	Salt and pepper

1	teaspoon seasoning salt
	Pinch of garlic powder
2	to 3 pounds round steak, cut into serving-size pieces
1	tablespoon vegetable oil
1	(4-ounce) can mushroom stems and pieces, diced
1	small onion, diced

➤ Combine the soup with half a soup can of water in a medium bowl. Add the steak sauce, ketchup, mustard, Worcestershire sauce, and sugar to taste. Mix well.

➤ Combine the flour, salt and pepper to taste, the seasoning salt, and garlic powder on a flat plate or in a plastic bag. Dredge the steak in the flour mixture.

➤ Heat the oil in a large skillet over medium heat. Add the steak pieces and quick-fry on both sides. Remove the meat from the pan and place in a slow cooker or an electric frying pan. Brown the mushrooms and onion in the oil remaining in the pan; then add them to the meat. Add the sauce.

➤ Cook for 10 to 12 hours on low in the slow cooker or about 3 hours in the electric frying pan. Serve with mashed potatoes and a vegetable.

Cook's Note: This recipe is great with venison, too.

ROSANNE M. MAYES
Holton, Michigan

"Don't Cry Daddy" Round Steak Sauerbraten

Yield: 6 servings

Elvis was stationed in Germany while he was in the army. He always liked good food and probably tried a version of this steak while he was there.

1½	**pounds (½-inch-thick) round steak**
1	**tablespoon canola or vegetable oil**
1	**(0.75-ounce) envelope brown gravy mix**
2	**cups water**
½	**teaspoon salt**
¼	**teaspoon pepper**
1	**bay leaf**
½	**teaspoon ground ginger**
1	**tablespoon minced onion**
2	**tablespoons white wine vinegar**
1	**teaspoon Worcestershire sauce**
2	**tablespoons brown sugar**
	Hot buttered noodles, for serving

➤ Cut the meat into 1-inch cubes. Heat the oil in a large skillet over medium-high heat. Brown the meat in the hot oil and remove it from the skillet. Add the gravy mix and water to the pan; bring to a boil, stirring constantly. Return the meat to the pan, and stir in the salt, pepper, bay leaf, ginger, onion, wine vinegar, Worcestershire sauce and brown sugar.

➤ Simmer, covered, 1½ hours or until the steak is tender, stirring occasionally. Remove the bay leaf. Serve the steak and gravy over the noodles.

SANDY WAREHIME
Amarillo, Texas
President, Elvis Friends Are the Best Friendship Circle

"Fever" Sandwiches

Yield: 8 to 10 sandwiches

1   (5 to 8-pound) chuck or rib-eye beef roast
    Salt and pepper
1   (10-ounce) jar pepperoncini, with their juice
8   to 10 hoagie buns

> Place the beef roast in a slow cooker. Add salt and pepper to taste. Add the pepperoncini, including the juice.

> Cover and cook on low for 8 to 10 hours or until the meat and pepperoncini are falling apart. Serve on hoagie buns.

Cook's Note: This dish may also be cooked on top of the stove in a heavy Dutch oven over low heat. Cook until the meat is falling apart. It will take up to 8 hours to cook on low.

SHERRY SHEAR
Memphis, Tennessee
Official Elvis Insider

Did You Know?

In the United States 150 of Elvis's albums and singles have gone gold, platinum, or multi-platinum.

Elvis the Mapmaker

Elvis was the unleashing of a revolution, and it was a revolution not only in terms of style. Elvis can properly be regarded, in my opinion, as a harbinger even of the integration movement.

"It's important to remember how 'unSouthern' American culture was then because of how utterly Southern it is now. There's really been what I think of as the 'Mississippification' of the whole culture. There weren't rib joints everywhere in 1954 or 1955; cornbread wasn't in everybody's diet on some level. And Elvis was part of the beginning of that and probably its chief cultural advanceman and exemplar in ways that went way beyond music to hair, clothes, attitudes, and accent. There was no other actor/entertainer of any prominence who kept the low Mississippi drawl he had. It was regarded as a pariah accent.

"He was a race-mixer at a time when that was a difficult and dangerous thing to be. He was appearing at black shows at the height of his initial fame in Memphis. People outside of Memphis didn't pay attention to it—in my opinion because the record company had no incentive to broadcast this because it was going to make him very controversial. And no one was showing any reportorial initiative because no one in the media understood how important he was, even though lots and lots of other people did.

"If you look at Ernest Withers' great pictures of him at the WDIA Christmas show in 1956 or 1957, you see that at that point he was a homeboy. The black people knew it and the white people knew it, and in that respect he is a harbinger of the integration movement; he really is.

"In the South, race relations were much more complicated and, in a certain sense, also much more open than in the North. In the North everything was hidden and bottled up and people never mingled. In the South, to some extent, everybody was living right around the corner from one another. As much as it was segregated by law, in reality it couldn't be. In a lot of ways, Elvis was taking something that had been in the dark and bringing it into the light, which is courageous.

"I think a lot of this has to do with Sam Phillips [founder of Sun Records and the producer of Elvis's first single, 'That's All Right,' in 1954]. I believe Sam was a reformer and wanted something like the result he got. And because of Sam's consciousness of that, Elvis had to be conscious of it. There was no way that Elvis didn't know what they were doing.

"Elvis was the one guy out there who was always the shining example of what you could get away with if you ignored all that information [about what you could or couldn't do, about social status and barriers]. The example he set of courage in moving beyond the imposed limitations was what Elvis was about, at least to me as an individual. And it was a job that had to be done by a white musician.

"If a black musician hit it, like Nat King Cole or Sam Cooke, the meaning was different and the barriers would still be up. They'd just come down for one specific individual. But then Elvis came along and the next thing you know we had Johnny Cash and Roy Orbison and Jerry Lee Lewis and Charlie Rich on the one side, and on the other side we had Little Richard and Chuck Berry. Everybody was coming out and things just started happening and coalescing.

"Little Richard has described Elvis a time or two as being like the guy at passport control who let him through to the other side in a foreign country. And that's correct because he kicked open a door out of the Deep South for a ton of people reaching all the way to Buddy Holly in Texas and Gene Vincent in Virginia. He wasn't just an individual, he was a catalytic individual, which is very different.

"He wasn't political; he wasn't Harry Belafonte or Sidney Poitier or even Marlon Brando; but he did know what he was doing, and he was comfortable with it.

"The truth of Elvis is that he was a liberator. Whether he meant it or he didn't mean it, whether he wished he had or wished he hadn't created the Beatles and Bob Dylan and whomever else—he did. He was a mapmaker, and the thing about Elvis was that you could trust his map."

DAVE MARSH,
Norwalk, Connecticut
Legendary rock music critic

"My Way" Cottage Pie

Yield: 4 to 6 servings

This pie is appetizing, nutritious, and fit for a king.

1½	**pounds potatoes, peeled and diced**
2	**leeks, sliced**
	Pat of butter
2	**ounces Cheddar cheese, grated, divided**
	Salt and pepper
1	**pound ground sirloin**
1	**onion, chopped**
2	**carrots, peeled and chopped**
2	**tablespoons all-purpose flour**
1	**cup beef stock**
1	**tablespoon tomato paste**
1	**tablespoon dried mixed herbs**

➤ Place the potatoes in a saucepan, cover with water, and cook on medium-high heat until tender. Add the leeks during the last 5 minutes of cooking time. Drain and mix with the butter and half the cheese. Season with salt and pepper to taste.

➤ Preheat the oven to 375 degrees. Lightly grease a 3-quart, ovenproof casserole.

➤ Sauté the beef, onion, and carrots in a medium skillet for 3 to 4 minutes over medium-high heat. Gradually add the flour, stock, tomato paste, and herbs. Bring to a boil and stir until thickened. Season with salt and pepper to taste, and spoon into the prepared ovenproof dish. Spread the potato mixture over the beef. Sprinkle the remaining cheese on top, and bake for 25 minutes or until golden on top.

PATRICIA KEERY
Lisburn Co. Antrim, North Ireland

"Burning Love" Tater Tot Casserole

Yield: 8 to 10 servings

This casserole will burn anyone's desire for love.

2	**pounds ground beef**
	Salt and pepper
	Garlic powder (optional)
	Onion powder (optional)
	Italian seasoning (optional)
	Red pepper (optional)
1	**cup chopped vegetables, such as carrots and onion (optional)**
1	**(32-ounce) package frozen tater tots**
1	**(10¾-ounce) can cream of mushroom or cream of celery soup**
1½	**cups shredded Cheddar cheese**

➤ Preheat the oven to 350 degrees. Grease a 9 x 12-inch baking dish.

➤ Brown the ground beef in a large skillet over medium-high heat. Add salt and pepper to taste and any optional seasonings or others of your choice. Stir in the vegetables, if desired; mix well.

➤ Place the tater tots and soup in the greased baking dish and mix well. Stir in the ground beef mixture.

➤ Bake for about 30 minutes or until the tater tots are browned. Add the shredded cheese and bake an additional 10 minutes or until the cheese is melted. Remove from the oven and cool 5 minutes before serving.

IRENE JANE HOLMES
Lynnwood, Washington
Angelish Fan Club

FROM ELVIS'S KITCHEN

Memories Meat Loaf

Yield: 8 servings

2	pounds ground beef
1	cup chopped onion
1	cup cored, seeded, and chopped green bell pepper
2	garlic cloves, chopped
3	large eggs
1	(4-ounce) package crackers, crushed
1	(8-ounce) can tomato sauce

MEATLOAF SAUCE

2	(8-ounce) cans tomato sauce
½	cup ketchup

➤ Preheat the oven to 350 degrees.

➤ Combine the ground beef, onion, bell pepper, garlic, eggs, crushed crackers, and tomato sauce in a large bowl. Mix well. Place in a large loaf pan and bake 1 hour, draining off any fat as needed.

➤ While the meatloaf is baking, make the sauce. Mix in a small bowl the tomato sauce and ketchup. Pour the Meatloaf Sauce over the meatloaf, return it to the oven, and bake an additional 15 minutes.

"Surrender" Best Ever Buttermilk Meat Loaf

Yield: 6 servings

This recipe from my mother-in-law makes you "surrender" all your good manners and just dig in.

1	**pound ground beef**
1	**large egg, lightly beaten**
½	**cup buttermilk**
½	**cup ketchup**
¾	**teaspoon salt**
	Black pepper
1	**teaspoon poultry seasoning**
½	**cup finely chopped onion**
½	**to ¾ cup cored, seeded, and finely chopped green bell pepper**
½	**cup unflavored breadcrumbs**
	Flour (optional)

➤ Preheat the oven to 350 degrees.

➤ Combine the ground beef with the egg in a large bowl. Mix in the buttermilk, ketchup, salt, pepper to taste, poultry seasoning, onion, bell pepper, and breadcrumbs. Pat the mixture into a 9 x 9-inch baking pan. Rub a small amount of flour on top of the loaf if desired.

➤ Bake for 45 minutes.

ROSILAN BROOKER
Waco, Texas
Memories of Elvis, Waco, Texas, fan club

"Promised Land" Hash

Yield: 8 to 10 servings

This hash is even better the second—or even the third—day.

3	**pounds ground beef**
5	**large onions, diced**
4	**to 5 potatoes, peeled and cut into cubes**
2	**tablespoons chili powder**
2	**cups ketchup**
½	**cup (1 stick) butter or margarine**
	Salt and pepper

➤ Brown the beef in a large skillet over medium-high heat. Add the onions, potatoes, chili powder, ketchup, butter, and salt and pepper to taste. Add just enough water to keep the mixture from sticking (too much water will make the hash soupy).

➤ Cook over medium heat until the potatoes are done, 45 minutes to 1 hour.

RUTH S. PIRKLE
Gainesville, Georgia
Official Elvis Insider

Elvis was often surrounded by beautiful women.

"Stay Away" Sloppy Joes

Yield: 8 Sloppy Joes

This tasty recipe from my childhood babysitter would have pleased Elvis and his friends.

1	**pound ground beef**
½	**cup chopped onion**
¼	**cup cored, seeded, and chopped green bell pepper**
¼	**cup chopped celery**
1	**(8-ounce) can tomato sauce**
¼	**cup ketchup**
1	**teaspoon pepper**
1	**tablespoon distilled white vinegar**
1	**tablespoon sugar**
1½	**tablespoons Worcestershire sauce**
	Salt
8	**hamburger buns**

➤ Combine the ground beef, onion, green pepper, and celery in a large skillet. Cook over medium-high heat until the beef has browned and the vegetables are tender.

➤ Combine the tomato sauce, ketchup, pepper, vinegar, sugar, Worcestershire sauce, and salt to taste in a medium bowl; mix well. Pour over the ground beef mixture in the skillet. Stir to combine.

➤ Simmer, covered, for 20 minutes. Serve on the hamburger buns.

CATHY WAGGONER
Webb City, Missouri
Return to Sender Club

FROM ELVIS'S KITCHEN

Cheeseburger

Yield: 1 burger

½   **pound ground beef**

3   **slices cheese**

4   **tablespoons (½ stick) butter**

1   **large hamburger bun**

1   **slice onion**

1   **slice tomato**

1   **lettuce leaf**

➤ Form the ground beef into a patty. Fry the hamburger in a medium skillet over medium-high heat until well done.

➤ Top with the cheese and cover the skillet until the cheese melts. Remove the patty from the pan.

➤ Drain any fat remaining in the pan, add the butter, and when it has melted, brown the bun halves on both sides. Place the patty on the bottom half of the toasted bun; add the onion, tomato, and lettuce, and cover with the top of the bun.

"Never Been to Spain" Spanish Delight

Yield: 8 servings

1	tablespoon vegetable oil
1	pound ground beef
1	large onion, minced
1	green bell pepper, cored, seeded, and chopped
1	(4-ounce) can sliced mushrooms, drained
1	(14.75-ounce) can whole-kernel corn, drained
1	(10¾-ounce) can tomato soup
1	(8-ounce) package wide egg noodles, cooked
8	ounces Cheddar cheese, shredded
	Salt and pepper

➤ Heat the oil over medium-high heat in a large skillet. Brown the ground beef, onion, and pepper in the oil; drain and return the meat to the pan. Stir the mushrooms, corn, and soup into the skillet with the meat mixture and simmer for 30 minutes, stirring occasionally.

➤ Add the noodles, cheese, and salt and pepper to taste; mix well. Cook for about 5 minutes or until the mixture is well blended and the cheese is melted.

JANE PERRY
Lufkin, Texas
Founding Member, Official Elvis Insider

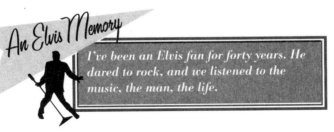

An Elvis Memory

I've been an Elvis fan for forty years. He dared to rock, and we listened to the music, the man, the life.

"Taking Care of Business®" Meat Loaf

Yield: 6 servings

Elvis would have been sure to be on time for this home-style favorite when the Graceland dinner bell rang—first to the table, and last to leave.

2	pounds ground chuck
1	medium onion, diced
1	medium green bell pepper, cored, seeded, and diced
3	large eggs
1	(16-ounce) can diced tomatoes and green chilies, drained
	Salt and pepper
1	cup ketchup
½	cup packed dark brown sugar
	Dash of Worcestershire sauce

➤ Preheat the oven to 375 degrees.

➤ In a large bowl combine the ground chuck, onion, bell pepper, eggs, and tomatoes and green chilies. Season with salt and pepper to taste. Mix well, making sure all ingredients are blended. Place the meat mixture in an 8 x 8-inch baking pan, leaving ½ inch around the sides. Bake for about 1 hour and 25 minutes or until done.

➤ While the meat is cooking, combine the ketchup, brown sugar, and Worcestershire sauce in a small bowl. Pour off any fat from the meatloaf and spread the brown sugar glaze over the top of the meatloaf for the final 10 minutes of cooking time.

LINDA CUNNINGHAM
Commerce, Texas

"All Shook Up" Hound Dogs

Yield: 1 dog

I hope someone introduced Elvis to a version of this wonderful treat when he came through Birmingham many years ago. Everyone who tries one becomes a fan.

2	cooked hot dogs, chopped
1	hot dog bun, chopped
1	teaspoon mustard
1	teaspoon ketchup
¼	cup chopped onion
15	oyster crackers
	Chili
	Coleslaw
	Shredded cheese (optional)

➤ Place the chopped hot dogs and buns in an oval banana split dish.

➤ Add the mustard, ketchup, onion, and oyster crackers. Top with the chili, coleslaw, and cheese, if desired.

LARRY JAMES
Birmingham, Alabama

Elvis and a "hound dog" pose.

With Elvis It Was More Personal

When you worked for Elvis, it wasn't just a typical job. A road manager normally just goes on the tours, sets up the tours, but I was also his right-hand man. I did everything that had to be organized for him, and that included everything—making reservations at restaurants, making sure everyone knew where he or she had to be at a certain time. For example, if he got up in the morning and said let's go to Palm Springs this afternoon, I'd get the jet ready, I'd call the crew, I'd call everyone who had to go, and I'd call California and say we were coming.

"We also vacationed together—that's a difference, too. We did everything together. We played together, we ate together, and we spent time with our families together. Vacation was often in Hawaii or in Colorado—we had friends in Colorado and we used to go there quite often—but mostly it was Hawaii, and Palm Springs, too.

"In Hawaii we'd stay at the Hilton Hawaiian Village on Oahu and then I'd rent a house on the other side of the island, on the beach at Kailua. We spent most of our days out there because it was a very quiet beach. The wives would make sandwiches and we'd picnic on the beach. It was a pretty normal vacation.

"When we were at Graceland, it didn't matter when you got up; if you wanted something to eat, they would make it for you. But a lot of the time they would have a lot of stuff prepared, like pot roast, fried chicken, mashed potatoes, gravy, pork chops, collard greens, fried okra, biscuits—anything you wanted, and a lot of fried foods. In the South they eat a lot of fried foods.

"At meals we'd all sit around and talk about normal guy stuff like sports or planning to do something. At breakfast sometimes his dad would come in and they'd discuss business, like house business. In the evening we'd just invite friends, and whoever was there was welcome to eat with us. There was always a good-size group around.

"We were careful where we went though. We'd tell the restaurants we were coming in, there'd be a private room, and we'd go in the back door. Sometimes we'd go to a place called Coletta's, an Italian pizza place. We'd go there and have pizzas, usually around 10 o'clock at night, before we'd go to the movies.

"During movies we'd have these little square White Castle hamburgers covered with grilled onions. We'd have one of the guys go out and get fifty or a hundred of them and give them to everyone in the movie theater. We'd sit and eat those. Our eating habits were not good, but we were young, and we didn't care.

"Elvis ate a lot of meatloaf and mashed potatoes—he liked meatloaf. For breakfast it was usually scrambled eggs and bacon and toast, or sometimes he'd have pancakes, but he had them with applesauce and butter instead of syrup.

"I used to make spaghetti sauce sometimes at the house on the West Coast because he liked spaghetti, and he liked my sauce. It's my secret family recipe. There are certain gimmicks about how you do it; it's not just the ingredients.

"In Vegas we ate dinner between shows. The first show was at eight. We'd eat at around ten or ten-thirty and the next show would be at twelve or twelve-thirty. We'd have a chef from one of the restaurants make something for all of us or else we'd have room service—cheeseburgers, club sandwiches, grilled cheese with bacon and tomato—basically whatever we wanted.

"In L.A. in the early sixties there was a place called the Luau on Rodeo Drive. It was beautiful inside with waterfalls and screens, and it was very popular—a show business hangout. They had a great hamburger steak that Elvis ordered smothered with grilled onions. It was delicious. I ate that myself.

"In Cleveland we stayed at a hotel called Swingos, which had a restaurant called The Keg and Quarter—I have no idea what that means, but it was a great restaurant. It was also a very famous hotel—Frank Sinatra and Dean Martin used to stay there too.

"And in Denver we went to a place called the Colorado Mining Company. It isn't there any more, but it was very popular in the seventies. Everybody knew us there and they didn't bother us.

"The road's a pretty boring thing, but the way we did it we kept pretty busy. We'd arrive in a town in the afternoon, get ready for the show, and do the show. And then right after the show we'd jump on our plane and go to the next town. That gave us time to unwind. By the time we got to the hotel it could be two o'clock in the morning. We'd sit around for a while and go to bed. The next day we'd get up and start all over again. It was boring at times—we'd sit around and watch television, watch sports, talk. We never saw what the town looked like. All we saw was the back door of the hotel, the back of the arena, and that was it.

"On the road, mostly it was room service, but in certain towns we had a lot of friends. In Philadelphia, as soon as we got into town we'd have Philly steak sandwiches—we'd have them waiting at the hotel for us. And there was one police officer who got us cannoli—homemade fresh cannoli. We'd have a helluva meal every time we got to Philly.

"We were very close, so sometimes we'd get upset with each other, like married couples do. But we had a good time. We had our own group. Elvis liked to have his friends around him."

JOE ESPOSITO,
El Dorado Hills, California
Elvis's high school friend and road manager

120

"Trying to Get to You" Porcupine Meatballs

Yield: 4 servings

This recipe reminds me of something Elvis would have had his cook prepare.

1   **large egg, beaten**
1   **(10¾-ounce) can condensed tomato soup, divided**
¼   **cup uncooked, long-grain rice**
2   **tablespoons finely chopped onion**
1   **tablespoon snipped parsley**
½   **teaspoon salt**
⅛   **teaspoon pepper**
1   **pound ground beef**
1   **tablespoon vegetable oil**
1   **teaspoon Worcestershire sauce**
½   **cup water**

➤ Combine the egg and ¼ cup of the soup in a medium bowl. Stir in the rice, onion, parsley, salt, and pepper. Add the ground beef, and mix well. Shape the mixture into 20 small balls.

➤ Heat the oil in a 10-inch skillet over medium heat. Lightly brown the meatballs and transfer them to paper towels to drain. Spoon the remaining soup into the skillet, add the Worcestershire sauce and water, and mix well. Return the meatballs to the skillet and simmer, covered, 30 to 35 minutes.

Cook's Note: Add 2 tablespoons brown sugar to the sauce, if you like, for additional flavor.

CHARLE REEVES
Okemah, Oklahoma
Elvis fan club of Oklahoma

"Viva Las Vegas" Pasta Dish

Yield: 4 to 6 servings

½   **tablespoon butter or margarine**
1   **small onion, chopped**
1   **pound hot dogs, cut up**
1   **(16-ounce) jar tomato sauce with meat**
2   **(14-ounce) cans stewed tomatoes**
1   **pound elbow macaroni**
    Salt and pepper

➤ Melt the butter in a large skillet over medium heat. Add the onion and sauté until tender. Add the hot dogs and cook until browned; then add the tomato sauce and tomatoes

➤ Cook the macaroni in a medium saucepan according to package directions; drain well. Spoon the pasta into a large bowl or platter. Pour the hot dogs and sauce over the pasta and mix well. Season with salt and pepper to taste.

LOIS ANN HOLBROOK
Showell, Maryland

Memphis Veal on a Stick

Yield: 4 servings

On hot nights, this is the perfect outdoor family treat.

3   **veal steaks, cut into 1-inch cubes**
2   **large eggs, well beaten**
1   **cup cracker crumbs**

    Salt and pepper
½   **cup vegetable oil**

➤ Thread the veal cubes onto four wooden skewers that have been soaked in water. Dip the skewered meat in the egg; then roll it in the cracker crumbs. Season with the salt and pepper to taste.

➤ Heat the oil in a large skillet over medium heat and fry the skewered meat until golden brown.

SUSAN ROBINSON
Jersey City, New Jersey

"One Night" Hamburger and Potato Casserole

Yield: 4 servings

1   **pound ground beef**
1   **medium onion, chopped**
3   **medium potatoes, peeled and sliced**
1   **(10¾-ounce) can cream of mushroom soup**

➤ Preheat the oven to 350 degrees. Grease a 9 x 13-inch baking dish.

➤ Brown the ground beef and onion in a medium skillet over medium-high heat; drain well. Alternate layers of the beef mixture and the potatoes in the prepared pan. Top with the soup.

➤ Bake for 45 minutes.

LEE ANN DAVIDSON AND CARLENE ELVIK
Garden City, South Dakota
Official Elvis Insider

"Coney Island" Hot Dogs with Hound Sauce

Yield: 10 servings

Elvis loved dogs, as shown by his appearance on *The Steve Allen Show* with the famous hound dog.

1	pound lean ground beef
2	cups canned tomatoes
1	garlic clove, minced
1	to 2 teaspoons chili powder
	Few drops of Tabasco sauce
	Salt and pepper
10	cooked hot dogs on buns
1	cup chopped onion
	Shredded cheese (optional)

➤ Brown the meat in a large skillet over medium heat, stirring with a fork to break it up. Add the tomatoes, garlic, chili powder, Tabasco, and salt and pepper to taste.

➤ Simmer the mixture, covered, 20 minutes or until the sauce has thickened. Spoon over the hot dogs and top with the chopped onion and cheese, if using.

ELISABET MCQUEEN
Parma, Ohio
Official Elvis Insider

"I'm a Roustabout" Chuck Roast

Yield: 2 to 4 servings

I think Elvis would have loved this dish because he was a lover of good home cooking.

1	**(3- to 4-pound) boneless chuck roast**
1	**(0.9-ounce) package onion soup mix**
1	**(10¾-ounce) can cream of mushroom soup**
½	**cup water**

➤ Preheat the oven to 350 degrees.

➤ Place the roast on a large sheet of heavy-duty aluminum foil. Sprinkle the onion soup mix over the meat (no salt or pepper is needed). Spoon the mushroom soup over the onion soup mix. Pour the water around the bottom of the meat. Cover with another large sheet of aluminum foil and seal all the edges.

➤ Place the foil package in a large pan or on a baking sheet. Bake for 3½ to 4 hours or until the meat is tender.

Cook's Note: Place cut carrots, celery, and potatoes alongside the meat if desired.

BEVERLY ESTEPP
Reading, Ohio
Official Elvis Insider

Viva La-S'getti

Yield: 6 to 8 servings

Just as folks came from far and wide to experience Elvis in Las Vegas, my friends and family can't wait to gather around my table for my signature dish. Like Elvis's music, which wasn't just rock and roll but mixed in with gospel, rhythm and blues, country, rockabilly, pop, and even soul, this dish offers a delicious, unique flavor that so many ingredients bring to the mix.

1	**pound ground beef**
¼	**teaspoon garlic salt**
1	**teaspoon sugar**
1	**teaspoon salt**
1	**teaspoon pepper**
2	**(8-ounce) cans tomato sauce**
¼	**cup chopped onion**
8	**to 10 ounces small pasta shells, uncooked**
1	**cup shredded Swiss cheese**
1	**cup shredded mozzarella cheese**
1	**(8-ounce) container sour cream**
1	**(3-ounce) package cream cheese, softened**
1	**cup shredded sharp Cheddar cheese**

➤ Preheat the oven to 350 degrees. Grease a 9 x 13-inch baking pan.

➤ Brown the meat in a large skillet; add the garlic salt, sugar, salt, pepper, tomato sauce, and onion. Cover and simmer 15 minutes.

➤ Cook the pasta shells just until tender; drain and pour them into the prepared baking pan. Sprinkle with the Swiss cheese. Pour the meat mixture over the noodle layer. Sprinkle with the mozzarella cheese.

➤ Combine the sour cream and cream cheese in a small bowl; spoon over the meat layer. Sprinkle with the sharp Cheddar cheese. Bake for 15 to 20 minutes or until the cheese melts.

CATHI COX
Ruston, Louisiana
Founding Member, Official Elvis Insider

Did You Know?

Elvis has sold more records than anyone else in record industry history.

"Change of Habit" Spaghetti Cake

Yield: 12 servings

1½	**pounds spaghetti**
6	**tablespoons butter or margarine**
1¼	**cups freshly grated Parmesan cheese**
6	**large eggs, well beaten**
3	**cups cottage cheese**
3	**pounds ground beef or bulk pork sausage**
1½	**cups chopped onion**
⅔	**cup cored, seeded, and chopped green bell pepper**
1	**(24-ounce) can tomatoes, cut up, with their liquid**
1	**(18-ounce) can tomato paste**
3	**teaspoons sugar**
3	**teaspoons crushed dried oregano**
1½	**teaspoons garlic salt**
2	**cups shredded mozzarella cheese**

➤ Cook the spaghetti according to package directions; drain well.

➤ Preheat the oven to 350 degrees. Grease a 9 x13-inch baking pan.

➤ Place the hot spaghetti in a large bowl and stir in the butter, Parmesan cheese, and eggs. Spoon the mixture into the prepared pan. Spread the cottage cheese on top.

➤ Brown the meat, onion, and green pepper in a large skillet over medium heat until the vegetables are tender and the meat is browned. Drain off the excess fat. Stir in the tomatoes with their liquid, the tomato paste, sugar, oregano, and garlic salt; heat thoroughly.

➤ Spread the meat mixture over the cottage cheese and bake the spaghetti cake, uncovered, for 25 minutes. Sprinkle the mozzarella cheese on top of the meat mixture. Bake for 5 minutes longer or until the cheese melts.

➤ Cool slightly and cut into squares to serve.

Cook's Note: Add more Italian spices if desired.

MARILYN HUDDLESTON
Waterloo, Illinois
Official Elvis Insider

An Elvis Memory

Elvis came to St. Louis in 1976. In order to get tickets, I had to take along my two-month-old son, whom I was nursing at the time. During the eight-hour wait in line, I nursed him twice, changed his diapers, and rocked him to sleep. My son got what he needed and so did I—those precious tickets.

"G.I. Blues" Brown Beef Gravy

Yield: 6 servings

This rich gravy would remind a G.I. of home cooking and the girl he left behind. It's good, yet so easy that even a bride could cook it. I made it up from bits and pieces of several recipes. Combining the butter with olive oil adds extra flavor. Elvis loved home cooking, and would have approved of this gravy, because it is plain cooking with a little something extra.

¼	**cup butter**
4	**tablespoons light olive oil**
1	**medium onion, thinly sliced**
4	**garlic cloves, thinly sliced**
½	**cup plus 2 tablespoons all-purpose flour**
1	**teaspoon salt**
1	**teaspoon freshly ground pepper**
½	**cup very dry cooking sherry**
2	**(10¾-ounce) cans beef broth**
2	**cups water**

➤ Heat the butter and olive oil in a 2-quart saucepan over medium-low heat. Add the onion and garlic and sauté until golden brown, stirring constantly. Add the flour, salt, and pepper and stir until the mixture is bubbly. Add the sherry slowly, stirring constantly. Add the beef broth and the water slowly, continuing to stir. Turn the heat up to medium and cook, stirring, until the mixture thickens a bit, about 5 minutes.

➤ Let the gravy stand about 5 minutes and then pour it through a fine sieve. Reserve the onions and garlic. Serve over sliced roast beef with the onions and garlic on top. The strained gravy is also great over mashed potatoes as a side dish.

SANDY STAEHLIN
Corvallis, Oregon
If I Can Dream Elvis Fan Club of Washington State

"Burning Love" Pepper Steak

Yield: 2 servings

Elvis loved red meat and rich foods, making this a perfect dish for him.

1	**(1½-pound) New York strip or 2 small rib-eye steaks**
2	**tablespoons green peppercorns in water, drained and crushed**
2	**tablespoons steak sauce**
2	**tablespoons water**
1	**cup heavy cream**
	Salt and pepper

Heat a cast-iron skillet over medium heat until a drop of water bounces off. Sprinkle the skillet lightly and evenly with salt. Add the steak and cook until it browns well, about 3 minutes; turn and brown the other side. The steak will be very rare. Remove to a warm plate and cover with foil.

Mix the peppercorns with the steak sauce and water. Pour into the hot skillet and deglaze, stirring and scraping up any browned pieces of steak sticking to the pan. Add the cream and let the gravy simmer on low. Season with the salt and pepper to taste.

Warm a serving dish by placing it in hot water or in the microwave oven. Cut the steak into sixteen strips. Return the sliced steak and any collected juices to the skillet. Bring the sauce to a boil, stirring until it thickens slightly. Cook the steak until it is done to your liking. Using a spatula, arrange the steak strips in the center of two dinner plates and pour the sauce over them.

Serve with sautéed potatoes, green beans, and French bread for a complete meal.

SANDI PICHON
Slidell, Louisiana

"The Lady Loves Me" Sunday Baked Ham

Yield: 12 to 15 servings

Elvis loved huge, heart-warming, family, sit-down meals, and this baked ham is a sure crowd-pleaser. It's simple and yummy.

2	tablespoons all-purpose flour	1	cup pineapple juice
1	cup firmly packed dark brown sugar	¼	cup distilled white vinegar
1	tablespoon prepared mustard	1	(8 to 10-pound) smoked ham shank

➤ Preheat the oven to 350 degrees.

➤ Combine the flour, brown sugar, mustard, pineapple juice, and vinegar in a small bowl; mix well. Place the ham in a large baking pan. Pour the flour mixture over the ham. Place a meat thermometer in the middle of the ham.

➤ Bake, basting every half hour, until the thermometer reaches 160 degrees, about 3½ hours.

GLENDA STAECEY
Colville, Washington

"Mean Woman Blues" Ribs

Yield: 4 to 6 servings

This good Southern pork chop variation is truly fit for a king.

3	cups ketchup	2	tablespoons Worcestershire sauce
½	cup molasses		Cayenne
2	tablespoons liquid smoke	3	pounds country-style pork ribs
½	cup firmly packed brown sugar	½	teaspoon garlic salt
2	tablespoons distilled white vinegar		Black pepper

➤ Combine the ketchup, molasses, liquid smoke, brown sugar, vinegar, Worcestershire sauce, and cayenne to taste in a large bowl. Cut the ribs into serving-size portions and place in a large Dutch oven. Add water to cover, the garlic salt, and black pepper to taste.

➤ Bring to a boil, cover, and reduce the heat. Simmer for 30 minutes. Drain well and grill the ribs over slow coals, brushing them with the sauce as they cook.

SANDI PICHON
Slidell, Louisiana
TCB Elvis Style

FROM ELVIS'S KITCHEN

Special Barbecue Sauce

Yield: about 5 cups

4	(8-ounce) cans tomato sauce	2	slices lemon
1	tablespoon soy sauce	1	tablespoon brown sugar
1	tablespoon dry mustard	2	tablespoons honey
1	tablespoon chili powder	1	tablespoon ground red pepper
½	cup distilled white vinegar	1	tablespoon pickling spices

➤ Combine the tomato sauce, soy sauce, mustard, chili powder, vinegar, lemon slices, brown sugar, honey, red pepper, and pickling spices in a medium saucepan; cook over low heat, stirring often, for 30 minutes.

➤ Serve with ribs, chicken, or pork.

"If I Could Dream"
Zucchini Casserole

Yield: 6 servings

This is fit for a king because he is getting his meat, potatoes, and vegetables all together. It's filling, so he can rock-a-hula all night long.

- 1   **pound ground beef**
- 1   **(16-ounce) jar spaghetti sauce, or more if you like it saucier**
- 2   **large potatoes, peeled and sliced**
- 1   **large onion, peeled and sliced**
- 1   **large zucchini, peeled and sliced**
     Freshly grated Parmesan cheese
     Shredded mozzarella cheese (optional)

➤ Brown the ground beef in a large skillet over medium heat and stir in the spaghetti sauce.

➤ Preheat the oven to 350 degrees. Grease a 9 x 9-inch baking dish.

➤ Place a layer of potatoes in the prepared dish, then a layer of onion, then a layer of zucchini. Add a layer of ground beef and sauce. Sprinkle with the Parmesan and, if desired, the mozzarella cheeses. Repeat the layers until all the ingredients are used, ending with the cheese.

➤ Bake for 1 hour or until the vegetables are tender. Cover with foil after 30 to 40 minutes if the casserole begins to burn on top.

SHARON CRISSMAN
New Bethlehem, Pennsylvania
Official Elvis Insider

"Rock-a-Hula" Ham

Yield: 4 to 6 servings

Elvis would have loved this versatile and tasty dish.

2	tablespoons vegetable oil
1	green bell pepper, cored, seeded, and coarsely chopped
1	red bell pepper, cored, seeded, and coarsely chopped
1	celery stalk, thinly sliced
1	carrot, peeled and thinly sliced
1	onion, chopped
	Salt and pepper
3	cups diced cooked ham
1	(8-ounce) can pineapple chunks
⅓	cup packed light brown sugar
1	teaspoon red wine or balsamic vinegar
1	tablespoon cornstarch
1	(10¾-ounce) can chicken broth
	Soy sauce (optional)
2	cups cooked rice

➤ Heat the oil in a large skillet over medium heat. Sauté the peppers, celery, carrot, and onion in the oil until tender. Season with the salt and pepper to taste.

➤ Add the diced ham. Drain the pineapple, reserving the juice. Add the pineapple to the skillet. Combine the brown sugar, vinegar, reserved pineapple juice, cornstarch, and chicken broth in a small bowl.

➤ Pour the mixture over the meat and vegetables, stirring until the sauce is thickened. Add the soy sauce to taste, if desired. Serve over cooked rice.

SUZANNE BURLEW
Cantonment, Florida
Official Elvis Insider

"Blue Hawaii" Sweet and Sour Hawaiian Spareribs

Yield: 6 to 8 servings

Serve this recipe with mashed potatoes, gravy, and Southern-style biscuits, and the old taste buds will stand up and shout, "Thankyou, thankyouverymuch!"

3	pounds boneless country-style pork ribs
	Salt and pepper
½	cup chopped onion
¼	cup cored, seeded, and chopped green bell pepper
2	(8-ounce) cans tomato sauce
1	teaspoon Worcestershire sauce
⅓	cup red wine vinegar
1	(8-ounce) can pineapple tidbits and juice
¼	cup packed light brown sugar
½	teaspoon dry mustard

➤ Preheat the oven to 350 degrees.

➤ Place the ribs in a roasting pan and season with salt and pepper to taste. Bake for 1 hour. Reduce the oven temperature to 300 degrees so the ribs do not burn and continue to bake for an additional 20 minutes.

➤ Combine the onion, bell pepper, tomato sauce, Worcestershire sauce, vinegar, pineapple with juice, brown sugar, and dry mustard in a medium bowl. Pour the mixture over the ribs and bake for an additional 45 minutes, basting often with the sauce.

HELEN GRANT
Mansfield, Texas

An Elvis Memory

I have been a fan from the very beginning of Elvis's career. His music has been a joy and therapy to my heart and soul. My grandchildren, Brittany and Christian, love to sing along with their favorite Elvis songs.

"Stuck on You" Sausage Scaloppini

Yield: 8 to 10 servings

This authentic Italian dish is appropriate for any king's table.

1	**tablespoon vegetable oil**
4	**green bell peppers, cored, seeded, and sliced**
2	**red bell peppers, cored, seeded, and sliced**
1	**medium onion, finely chopped**
1	**pound mushrooms, sliced**
2	**garlic cloves, minced**
3	**pounds sweet Italian sausage**
1	**pound hot Italian sausage**
1	**plus ½ cups water**
3	**(16-ounce) cans tomato sauce**

➤ Heat the oil in a large skillet over medium heat. Add the peppers, onion, mushrooms, and garlic, and sauté until tender but not brown.

➤ Transfer the vegetables to a large stockpot. Place the hot and sweet sausages in the skillet with the ½ cup water. Cook completely.

➤ Remove the sausages and cut into bite-size pieces. Add the sausages to the stockpot along with the tomato sauce and the remaining 1 cup water.

➤ Cook on medium heat about 1 hour, stirring occasionally. Serve over pasta or rice, or as a sandwich on a hard Italian roll.

NANCY VIETRO
Clementon, New Jersey

"Big Boss Man"
Italian Sausage Bombers

Yield: 10 servings

Ever since the first time I served this at an Elvis fan-club meeting, the members have been asking me to make it again.

2	pounds mild or hot Italian sausage		2	(29-ounce) cans tomato sauce
2	medium onions, sliced		¾	cup water
2	large green bell peppers, cored, seeded and chopped into 1¼-inch pieces			Salt and pepper
			10	hoagie or bomber buns

➤ Brown the sausage well in a large skillet over medium-high heat; drain and return the meat to the pan. Add the onions and green peppers and cook until the vegetables are tender. Add the tomato sauce, water, and salt and pepper to taste.

➤ Simmer, covered, for about 2 hours. Serve on the buns.

MARY R. HEIDTMAN
Kenosha, Wisconsin
Forever Elvis Fan Club of Wisconsin

Six

Poultry
and
Seafood

Graceland's Table

"Little Sister" Chicken and Rice

"I Got Stung" Pepper Chicken

"I'm Coming Home" Chicken and Dressing

"Don't Cry Daddy," It's Chicken and Dressing

Pistachio-Crusted Chicken Breasts

"It's Easy for You" Coconut Chicken

"Moody Blues" Chili Chicken

"Burning Love" Chicken Enchilada Casserole

Chicken Karahi

"Too Much" Home-Style Fried Chicken

"Thank You, Thank You Very Much" Chicken

Rock-a-Hula Haystack

Grilled Vodka-Marinated Shrimp

Super-Rich Crab Cakes

Pan-Sautéed Fish Fillets

Mediterranean Sea Bass

Georgia Peanut-Crusted Halibut

Boneless Chicken

"Little Sister" Chicken and Rice

Yield: 4 servings

This recipe reminds me of Elvis—irresistible: Once you've had a taste, you'll always come back for more.

8	**chicken thighs**
	Salt and pepper
4	**teaspoons mild curry powder**
3	**tablespoons vegetable oil**
1½	**tablespoons sugar**
1	**large onion, finely chopped**
2	**garlic cloves, crushed**
1	**(8-ounce) can chopped tomatoes**
4	**cups water, or as needed**
1	**cup uncooked long-grain rice**

➤ Rinse the chicken; season with the salt and pepper to taste and the curry powder. Refrigerate for 2 hours.

➤ Heat the oil in a large skillet over high heat and stir in the sugar. When the sugar turns golden brown and starts to smoke, add the chicken and gently shake the pan. After 5 minutes, turn the chicken to make sure all sides are coated. Cook 15 minutes, turning occasionally, and then add the onion and garlic. Cook 5 minutes and then add the tomatoes. Cook an additional 5 minutes. Add just enough water to cover the chicken. Taste the sauce and add a little more salt if you wish. Bring to a boil, reduce the heat, and simmer for 30 minutes.

➤ While the chicken is simmering, cook the rice according to the package directions. Serve the chicken over the rice.

SONJA TIETJEN
Worthing, West Sussex, England
Official Elvis Insider

"I Got Stung" Pepper Chicken

Yield: 6 servings

My family members are meat eaters, as was Elvis. This would have been a favorite of his since it has many zesty ingredients.

6	boneless, skinless chicken breasts
1	tablespoon vegetable oil
1	tablespoon butter or margarine
⅓	cup chopped onion
½	green bell pepper, cored, seeded, and chopped
½	red bell pepper, cored, seeded, and chopped
1	(8-ounce) can tomato sauce
1	(16-ounce) can diced tomatoes with chilies
1	tablespoon sugar
1½	cups uncooked rice
⅛	teaspoon garlic salt
⅛	teaspoon salt
⅛	teaspoon pepper
1	cup water

➤ Preheat the oven to 350 degrees. Grease a 9 x 13-inch baking dish.

➤ Brown the chicken breasts in the oil in a large skillet. Remove the chicken from the pan. Melt the butter in the pan and sauté the onion, green pepper, and red pepper until tender.

➤ Pour the tomato sauce, tomatoes, and sugar into the prepared baking dish. Add the rice and stir well. Lay the browned chicken over the rice. Spread with the sautéed vegetables. Season with the garlic salt, salt, and pepper. Pour the water over all and bake, covered, for 45 minutes or until the rice is cooked and the chicken is tender. Add more water during baking if needed.

Cook's Note: You can substitute steak or pork chops for the chicken.

ROSILAN BROOKER
Waco, Texas
Memories of Elvis, Waco, Texas, fan club

The Guitar Was Bigger Than He Was

My father, Tracy Franks, was principal of the East Tupelo school, where Elvis went to elementary school. Back then, he was just a scrawny little kid who loved to sing and play the guitar, and my father let him sing at chapel. In those days, school started every morning with chapel, and every morning Elvis got up and sang "Old Shep," a song that was the signature of Gene Steele, a country singer on the Memphis radio station. I remember listening to the radio while I got dressed to go to school in the morning and then going to school crying each morning because Old Shep died.

"My father also let Elvis sing at every program the school put on. And sometimes, even though I went to a different school, I'd go to those programs and see him perform. At the time, I don't believe anyone would have thought he'd do anything. The guitar was bigger than he was, and he certainly didn't seem like any kind of prodigy. But he sure tried—and he certainly succeeded."

BOBBYE JONES
Tupelo, Mississippi

The Presley family was close knit.

"I'm Coming Home" Chicken and Dressing

Yield: 6 to 8 servings

I can envision Elvis's mama or Dodger making chicken and dressing for the family's Sunday dinners. My Mammaw's recipe carries with it those great memories of conversations at the table, singing around the piano, and kids playing in the yard. (Of course, Mammaw made her cornbread from scratch.)

1	(2½ to 3-pound) chicken
2	(15-ounce) packages white cornbread mix
1	medium onion
½	celery stalk
2	slices white bread

1	teaspoon salt
1	teaspoon pepper
2	teaspoons poultry seasoning
2	large eggs, lightly beaten
½	(10¾-ounce) can cream of chicken soup

➤ Cut up the chicken and boil very slowly until the meat is falling off the bones. Remove the meat and discard the bones. Save the cooking broth.

➤ Prepare and bake the cornbread according to package directions; set aside to cool.

➤ Chop the onion and celery in a blender. Transfer them to a small saucepan, add a small amount of water, and cook for a few minutes over medium-high heat, just until tender.

➤ Preheat the oven to 400 degrees.

➤ Crumble the cornbread and white bread into a very large mixing bowl. Add the salt, pepper, poultry seasoning, and onion mixture. Mix in the eggs. Mix the soup with ¼ cup of the reserved cooking broth and add it to the bread mixture. Pour the additional broth into the mixture to make it the consistency of cornbread mix or a little thinner. Add the chicken and stir well. Spoon the mixture into a 9 x 13-inch baking pan and bake for 30 to 40 minutes or until well browned on top.

Cook's Notes: You can cook the chicken and dressing until just bubbly in the center and then freeze. When ready to serve, thaw completely and bake 30 to 40 minutes.

JANE PERRY
Lufkin, Texas
Founding member, Official Elvis Insider

"Don't Cry Daddy," It's Chicken and Dressing

Yield: 6 to 8 servings

6	**chicken breasts cooked and chopped**
1	**(10¾-ounce) can chicken broth**
1	**(6-ounce) box instant stuffing mix**
¼	**cup chopped onion**
¼	**cup chopped celery**
1	**(10¾-ounce) can cream of mushroom soup**
1	**(10¾-ounce) can cream of chicken soup**
1	**(8-ounce) container sour cream**
1	**cup slivered almonds**

➤ Preheat the oven to 350 degrees. Grease a 9 x 13-inch baking dish.

➤ Combine the chicken, chicken broth, stuffing mix, onion, celery, soups, and sour cream in a large bowl. Spoon the mixture into the prepared baking dish. Top with the almonds and bake for 30 to 40 minutes or until well heated.

CATHY WAGGONER
Webb City, Missouri
Return to Sender Club

Pistachio-Crusted Chicken Breasts

Yield: 4 servings

1	**pound boneless, skinless chicken breasts**
1	**cup milk**
1	**large egg**
1	**cup pistachios, crushed**
	Dash of salt and black pepper

➤ Preheat the oven to 350 degrees. Spray a baking sheet with nonstick vegetable spray.

➤ Wash the chicken breasts and pat dry. Beat the milk and egg together in a small bowl. Combine the pistachios and salt and pepper on a flat plate. Dip the chicken breasts into the milk mixture and then coat both sides with the pistachios.

➤ Lay the chicken in the prepared pan and bake for about 30 minutes. Turn and bake an additional 10 minutes.

Cook's Note: For a crisper coating, broil the breasts for about 2 minutes on each side after baking.

PAULA M. POST
Boca Raton, Florida

The King of Rock & Roll with fans.

"It's Easy for You" Coconut Chicken

Yield: 4 to 6 servings

I believe that if Elvis were with us right now, he would love to try all these recipes, but he is still looking down on us as we are cooking and making our decisions in life.

- **1   cup all-purpose flour**
- **1   plus ½ cups coconut flakes**
- **1   cup chopped almonds**
- **2   cups graham cracker crumbs**
- **4   to 6 skinless, bone-in chicken breasts**
- **3   large eggs, lightly beaten**
-      **Vegetable oil, for frying**

➤ Preheat the oven to 350 degrees.

➤ Spread the flour on a large plate. On a second plate or a piece of aluminum foil, combine 1 cup coconut flakes, the almonds, and the graham cracker crumbs. Coat both sides of the chicken first with the flour, then the egg, and then the coconut mixture.

➤ Heat the oil in a large skillet over medium-high heat. Brown the chicken lightly in the hot oil on all sides. Transfer the breasts to a 9 x 13-inch baking pan and bake for 40 to 45 minutes or until golden brown.

➤ Remove the pan from the oven and sprinkle with the remaining ½ cup coconut before serving.

CAYCE MOLLYCHECK, AGE 13
Riverview, Florida

"Moody Blues" Chili Chicken

Yield: 6 to 8 servings

My taste in people and food is great. Elvis was a hot "dish," and I think he would have liked this hot dish.

1	**(16-ounce) package noodles**
2	**tablespoons butter or margarine**
½	**cup chopped onion**
2	**tablespoons finely chopped pickled jalapeño chile peppers**
3	**(10½-ounce) cans cream of mushroom soup**
1	**(4-ounce) can pimientos, chopped**
4	**cups chopped cooked chicken**
3	**cups shredded sharp Cheddar cheese, divided**
	Salt and pepper

➤ Preheat the oven to 325 degrees.

➤ In a large saucepan cook the noodles until tender, according to the package directions.

➤ In a large skillet melt the butter over medium heat. Add the onion and chile peppers and cook until the onion is tender. Add the soup and pimientos; simmer for 5 minutes.

➤ Grease an 8 x 13-inch baking dish. Layer with the chicken, half the cheese, half the soup mixture, and the noodles. Add the remaining soup mixture and top with the remaining cheese. Season with salt and pepper to taste and bake for 30 to 40 minutes or until the cheese melts.

PINKIE CARRENDER
Henley, Missouri

"Burning Love" Chicken Enchilada Casserole

Yield: 6 to 8 servings

This may not have been Elvis's typical food choice, but my favorite guy, who is so good at singing Elvis's songs, loves it.

9	**to 12 corn tortillas**
1	**to 1½ pounds cooked chicken, cubed or shredded**
1	**(14½-ounce) can green enchilada sauce (mild)**
1	**(14½-ounce) can red enchilada sauce (hot)**
1	**(14-ounce) can chicken broth**
1	**(8-ounce) can chopped green chilies**
1	**(16-ounce) package shredded Cheddar cheese**
	Chopped green onion and sour cream, for garnish

➤ Preheat the oven to 350 degrees.

➤ Tear the tortillas into medium-size pieces and spread them in the bottom of a 10 x 15-inch baking pan. Layer the chicken on top of the tortillas. Combine the enchilada sauces, chicken broth, and green chilies in a medium bowl. Pour the mixture over the chicken and tortillas.

➤ Cover with the cheese and bake, uncovered, for 45 to 60 minutes. Serve with chopped green onion and sour cream on the side.

Cook's Note: For added flavor and texture, fry the tortillas quickly before tearing them.

KAREN WRIGHT
Littleton, Colorado
Elvis Connection, Colorado

Chicken Karahi

Yield: 5 servings

This is an easy nutritious recipe that develops soft and gentle feelings in our hearts. It also gives us energy to lead active lives. I believe it is fit for the King of Rock and Roll.

3	tablespoons cooking oil
5	pounds boneless, skinless chicken breasts, cut up
1	tablespoon ground ginger
1	tablespoon garlic paste
1	tablespoon onion paste
1	tablespoon tomato paste
1	teaspoon salt
1	teaspoon red chili powder
1	teaspoon ground coriander
½	teaspoon ground turmeric
4	small green chilies, chopped
1	teaspoon black pepper

➤ Heat the cooking oil in a Dutch oven over medium-high heat. Add the chicken pieces and sauté for 2 minutes to brown slightly. Reduce the heat to medium and add the ginger, garlic, onion, and tomato paste; stir well to coat. Add the salt, chili powder, coriander, and turmeric; stir well to coat.

➤ Continue cooking the chicken for about 10 minutes, stirring often so the spices do not caramelize and burn. Stir in the green chilies, cover, and cook for 2 minutes. Sprinkle with the black pepper. Serve with bread and a salad.

Cook's Note: To make sure you get all the flavors, after removing the ingredients from the pan, add a small amount of chicken broth and use a wooden spoon to deglaze the pan, scraping up the browned bits from the bottom. Add this to the chicken before serving.

ZARTASHA SHAH
Conroe, Texas

"Too Much" Home-Style Fried Chicken

Yield: 4 to 6 servings

It's lip-smacking good!

½	cup (1 stick) butter, melted
3	cups self-rising flour
2	(0.6-ounce) packets Italian salad dressing mix
2	(1.25-ounce) packets tomato soup mix
1	teaspoon salt
1	(2 to 2½-pound) chicken, cut up

➤ Preheat the oven to 350 degrees. Spread the melted butter in the bottom of an 11 x 14-inch baking dish.

➤ Combine the flour, dressing mix, soup mix, and salt in a plastic bag; shake to mix well. Add the chicken, a few pieces at a time, and coat well before placing in the prepared pan.

➤ Bake for 30 minutes. Turn the chicken and bake for 30 minutes longer or until cooked through.

CINDY BROWN BROOKS
Greenville, Texas

Did You Know?

Elvis has sold more than a billion records worldwide.

"Thank You, Thank You Very Much" Chicken

Yield: 4 servings

I don't have memories of meeting or seeing Elvis in person because I was only six months old when he died. However, I have loved him since I was a little girl, and I want to say, "Thank you, thankyouverymuch for keeping his memory alive."

2	**large eggs**
2	**cups all-purpose flour**
2	**cups vegetable oil**
4	**chicken leg quarters**
2	**cups cooked rice**
1	**(10¾-ounce) can cream of mushroom soup**
1	**red bell pepper, cored, seeded, and sliced**

➤ Preheat the oven to 400 degrees. Lightly grease a 9 x 13-inch baking pan.

➤ Beat the eggs in a medium bowl. Place the flour in a separate bowl. Heat the oil in a large skillet on medium-high heat. Dip the chicken in the eggs, then in the flour. Cook the chicken in the hot oil until browned on both sides but not cooked through.

➤ Combine the rice and the soup and pour the mixture into the prepared pan. Place the browned chicken over the rice. Pour the skillet drippings over the chicken. Arrange the red pepper slices over the top of the chicken.

➤ Bake for 30 to 40 minutes or until the chicken is well done.

JILL HARDEN
Martinez, Georgia

Rock-a-Hula Haystack

Yield: 6 servings

You will find only the finest to tempt every palate served upon Graceland's table, from hors d'oeuvre to soup to salad. This entrée was made with the islands in mind, and just like the King, it is one of a kind.

1	**to 2 pounds ground turkey**
1	**(7.2-ounce) package Rice-A-Roni Herb & Butter, cooked and cooled**
2	**large eggs**
3	**(10¾-ounce) cans cream of mushroom soup**
	Freshly grated Parmesan cheese
	Pineapple chunks, for garnish

➤ Preheat the oven to 350 degrees.

➤ Combine the turkey with the cooked rice. Add the eggs, mix well, and shape into large meatballs. Pour the soup into the bottom of a 9 x 13-inch baking dish. Place the meatballs in the soup. Bake, covered, for 1 hour.

➤ Remove the cover, sprinkle with the Parmesan cheese, and bake for 15 minutes longer. Serve with the pineapple chunks to add a bit of island flavor.

Cook's Note: Ground beef can be substituted for the turkey.

SHANNON PELLETIER SWANSON
Apopka, Florida

I Was Expecting
It to Look Like Tara

When I knew I'd be talking to you, I called my sister to verify that I hadn't always been this way, and she assured me that she wasn't aware of my Elvis obsession when we were growing up. I'd seen all the Elvis movies, of course, but I didn't really become a full-blown devotee until I was a grown—shall we say 'mature'—woman. In fact, I think it really began the first time I went to Graceland, which was probably in 1989 or 1990.

"The whole Graceland experience was just so intense. I remember buying these Elvis stickers in the gift shop that I started putting on envelopes for a while—that really shocked some of my friends. Actually, I think it still surprises people when they find out that I'm an older, generally conservative, African-American woman who loves Elvis. Somehow it just doesn't fit everything else they know about me.

"In any case, the first time I went to Graceland (I've been there twice now.) I didn't really know what to expect, but I probably thought it would be some kind of mansion—maybe like Tara. And even though it's a nice house, and it does have a portico with white pillars, what really impressed me about it was the inside. It wasn't just the room where all the costumes are displayed. It was more that all the rooms looked exactly as if Elvis were still living there. I can see why people can't believe he's dead. I think his spirit may actually still be living at Graceland."

BRENDA RHODES MILLER
Washington, D.C.

Grilled Vodka-Marinated Shrimp

Yield: 4 servings

1½   **pounds large uncooked shrimp, peeled and deveined**
1   **plus ½ cups vodka**
1   **small fresh lemon or lime**
    Freshly ground black pepper

▷ Place the shrimp in a medium bowl. Cover with 1 cup vodka and marinate in the refrigerator for 12 hours.

▷ Before grilling the shrimp, mix the remaining ½ cup vodka with the juice from the lemon or lime and freshly ground black pepper to taste. Place in the freezer for about 30 minutes.

▷ Remove the shrimp from the vodka marinade and grill outdoors or in a grill pan until the shrimp turn pink; turn and grill quickly on the opposite side. Serve the vodka and juice mixture as a dipping sauce.

ED MCDONOUGH
Menton, France

Graceland was his true home.

Super-Rich Crab Cakes

Yield: 4 servings

2	cups backfin crabmeat (about ¾ pound), picked over
1½	cups fresh breadcrumbs
2	large eggs
½	cup heavy cream
	Dash of hot sauce (or to taste)
2	teaspoons Worcestershire sauce
2	teaspoons chopped fresh parsley leaves
2	teaspoons grated onion
	Salt and pepper
1	plus 1 tablespoons unsalted butter

Combine the crabmeat and breadcrumbs in a medium bowl. Whisk the eggs in a small bowl and whisk in the cream. Add the cream mixture, hot sauce, Worcestershire sauce, parsley, onion, and salt and pepper to taste to the crab mixture; combine well.

Melt 1 tablespoon of the butter in a skillet over moderate heat; then drop in half the crab mixture by the tablespoonful. Cook the crab cakes until golden brown, about 2 minutes, on each side. Repeat with the 1 remaining tablespoon butter and the remaining crab mixture. Serve warm.

PAULA M. POST
Boca Raton, Florida

Pan-Sautéed Fish Fillets

Yield: 2 servings

1	**small lemon or lime**
1	**pound thin fish fillets, such as snapper, tilapia, orange roughy, or cod**
1	**cup cornmeal**
½	**teaspoon cayenne**
¼	**teaspoon ground cumin**
	Salt and pepper
2	**tablespoons vegetable oil**
1	**tablespoon butter**

➤ Squeeze the juice of the lemon or lime over the fillets. Combine the cornmeal, cayenne, cumin, and salt and pepper to taste on a flat plate or a sheet of wax paper. Dredge the fillets in the cornmeal mixture.

➤ Heat the oil and butter in a large skillet over medium-high heat and sauté the fillets until golden on both sides. Serve with "Burning Love" Watermelon Salsa (page 20).

JOHN BOKER
Irvine, California

Did You Know?

*Elvis dressed in a tuxedo
and sang "Hound Dog" to a basset hound
on The Steve Allen Show in 1956.*

Mediterranean Sea Bass

Yield: 4 servings

¼	**cup lemon juice**
4	**plus 2 tablespoons olive oil**
	Salt and pepper
1½	**to 2 pounds sea bass fillets**
¼	**red onion, thinly sliced**
1	**garlic clove, chopped**
1	**medium tomato, seeded and chopped**
¼	**cup coarsely chopped green or black olives**
¼	**cup coarsely chopped fresh basil leaves**
2	**tablespoons finely chopped parsley**
1	**tablespoon drained capers**

➤ Combine the lemon juice, 4 tablespoons olive oil, and salt and pepper to taste in a large sealable plastic bag. Add the sea bass fillets and marinate for about 10 minutes.

➤ While the fish marinates, heat the remaining 2 tablespoons of olive oil in a medium skillet over medium heat. Sauté the red onion and garlic in the oil until softened. Add the tomato and olives and cook 1 minute. Season with salt and pepper to taste.

➤ Heat a grill pan. Remove the fillets from the marinade and grill on one side 4 to 5 minutes or until brown; turn and cook on the opposite side about 3 minutes or until the fish is cooked through.

➤ Toss the onion and garlic mixture with the basil, parsley, and capers and serve over the fish.

VICKIE BIEHL
Kutztown, Pennsylvania

Georgia Peanut-Crusted Halibut

Yield: 2 servings

1	fresh lemon or lime
2	(6-ounce) halibut fillets
½	cup breadcrumbs
¼	cup all-purpose flour
	Salt and pepper
½	teaspoon ground cumin
½	teaspoon ground cinnamon
½	teaspoon paprika
½	cup finely chopped roasted peanuts
2	tablespoons olive oil
1	tablespoon butter

➤ Squeeze the juice of the lemon or lime over the fillets. Combine the breadcrumbs, flour, salt and pepper to taste, cumin, cinnamon, paprika, and peanuts on a large flat plate or a sheet of wax paper. Dredge the fillets in the peanut mixture, pressing it into the fillets.

➤ Heat the oil and butter in a medium skillet over medium-high heat, and sauté the fish on one side for 4 to 5 minutes; turn and sauté another 3 minutes or until brown on the bottom.

Cook's Note: Serve over a bed of mixed greens seasoned with salt and pepper and tossed with olive oil and balsamic vinegar.

CYNTHIA EITNIER
Atlanta, Georgia

FROM ELVIS'S KITCHEN

Boneless Chicken

Yield: 4 servings

2   **tablespoons all-purpose flour**
1   **tablespoon black pepper**
1   **tablespoon seasoning salt**
4   **boneless, skinless chicken breasts**
½   **cup (1 stick) butter**

➤ Mix the flour, black pepper, and seasoning salt in a small bowl. Dredge both sides of the chicken breasts in the flour mixture.

➤ Melt the butter in a medium skillet over medium-high heat and fry the chicken breasts until they are cooked through and browned on both sides, about 7 minutes per side.

A photo of Elvis off the set while rehearsing for a concert that was filmed for the movie *That's the Way It Is*.

Seven

Soups
and
Stews

Graceland's Table

"I Got Stung" Sweet Potato Soup

"Spanish Eyes" Enchilada Chicken Soup

"Bossa Nova" Tortilla Soup, Baby

"El Toro" Taco Soup

"By and By" Potato Soup

"On a Snowy Winter Night" Slow Cooker Clam Chowder

"Treat Me Like a Fool" Salmon Stew

Charro's Cowboy Stew

"It's Impossible" Vegetable Beef Stew

"You Give Me Fever" Gumbo

"King Creole" Shrimp Creole

"I Got Stung" Sweet Potato Soup

Yield: 5 servings

A Southern-inspired holiday favorite.

¼	**cup (½ stick) butter**
1	**medium onion, chopped**
1	**teaspoon dried thyme**
4	**medium sweet potatoes, peeled and cubed**
5	**cups vegetable stock**
½	**cup firmly packed brown sugar**
6	**tablespoons heavy cream**

➤ Melt the butter in a Dutch oven over medium heat. Add the onion and cook until softened. Add the thyme and sweet potatoes and cook for 5 minutes. Add the stock and simmer until the sweet potatoes are soft.

➤ Remove from the heat and, when cool, transfer the soup to a blender or food processor and purée. Return the soup to the pot and stir in the brown sugar and heavy cream. Reheat to serve.

TOM BARTHEL
Long Beach, California

"Spanish Eyes" Enchilada Chicken Soup

Yield: 3 to 4 servings

Elvis would have loved this soup after a long, hard day of recording.

1	**(10¾-ounce) can nacho cheese soup**
1	**(10¾-ounce) can cream of chicken soup**
2⅔	**cups milk**
2	**cups cooked, boned chicken**
1	**(10-ounce) can enchilada sauce (red or green)**
½	**cup grated Monterey Jack cheese**
1	**cup chopped onion**
	Fried tortilla strips (optional)
	Salsa (optional)
	Sour cream (optional)

➤ Combine the soups, milk, chicken, and enchilada sauce in a heavy saucepan and mix well.

➤ Cook over medium heat, stirring often, until hot and smoking. Serve the soup topped with the grated cheese and onion. You can also add tortilla strips, salsa, and sour cream to the toppings if desired.

Cook's Note: Using green enchilada sauce will make a milder soup; red will make it hotter.

VICKY MITCHELL
Houston, Texas

"Bossa Nova" Tortilla Soup, Baby

Yield: 4 to 6 servings

In *Fun in Acapulco,* Elvis sang "Take it easy baby. I worked all day and my feet feel just like lead." That's how many of us feel when we get home at the end of the day. This soup is ideal—easy to make and hearty to boot. It will have you ready to rumba in no time at all.

2	**(10¾-ounce) cans cream of chicken soup**
1	**(10-ounce) can tomatoes with chilies (Rotel)**
2	**(14-ounce) cans chicken broth**
1½	**chicken breasts, cooked and boned** **(2 to 3 small cans of cooked chicken can be substituted)**
1	**(15-ounce) can ranch-style beans, drained**

➤ Blend the cream of chicken soup with the tomatoes with chilies in an electric blender. Transfer the mixture to a heavy saucepan and add the chicken broth. Stir in the chicken and beans and heat thoroughly over low heat.

➤ Serve this soup with taco salad and Mexican cornbread for a hearty meal.

Cook's Note: To serve, spoon the soup over tortilla chips or serve crushed tortilla chips as a garnish along with grated cheese and chopped green onions. For a thicker soup, use only 1 can of broth.

CATHI COX
Ruston, Louisiana
Founding member, Official Elvis Insider

"El Toro" Taco Soup

Yield: 8 to 10 servings

When the weather started to get cool, we rushed home from school knowing that Mom would have this soup waiting for us.

2	pounds ground beef	3	(16-ounce) cans stewed tomatoes, with liquid
1	large onion, chopped		
	Salt and pepper	2	(16-ounce) cans pinto or kidney beans, with liquid
1	(4-ounce) can chopped green chilies	2	(16-ounce) cans whole-kernel corn, with liquid
1	package taco seasoning		
1	package ranch salad dressing mix		

➤ Brown the beef in a large Dutch oven over medium-high heat. Add the onion and sauté until tender. Season with the salt and pepper to taste.

➤ Add the green chilies, taco seasoning, salad dressing mix, stewed tomatoes, kidney beans, and corn. Lower the heat to medium and cook, covered, for 30 minutes. Serve with taco chips or strips.

JEANIE NORRIS
Waco, Texas
Memories of Elvis, Waco, Texas, fan club

"By and By" Potato Soup

Yield: 4 to 6 servings

8	large potatoes, peeled and sliced	Salt and pepper
1	cup cubed Velveeta cheese	Minced chives or green onion, for garnish
	Milk, as needed	

- In a pot, cover the potatoes with water, bring to a boil, and cook until done. Mash the potatoes in their cooking water. Thoroughly mix in the cheese and enough milk to create a good soupy consistency.

- Season with salt and pepper to taste and cook over low heat to avoid scorching. Serve garnished with chives or green onion.

CINDY BROWN BROOKS
Greenville, Texas

"On a Snowy Winter Night" Slow Cooker Clam Chowder

Yield: 8 to 10 servings

I can see Elvis and his family sitting around the Graceland dining table on a cold winter night enjoying this hearty chowder with freshly baked biscuits.

1	medium onion, diced
1	plus 1 tablespoons butter
4	large potatoes, peeled and diced
4	slices bacon, diced and fried
2	bay leaves
3	(10-ounce) cans baby clams, with juice
2	(10¾-ounce) cans cream of celery soup
3	carrots, peeled and diced
⅓	cup all-purpose flour
1	cup heavy cream
½	cup milk
	Salt and pepper

- In a small skillet over medium heat sauté the onion in 1 tablespoon butter until translucent but not browned. Combine the potatoes, bacon, bay leaves, clams and clam juice, soup, and carrots in a slow cooker.

- Cook, covered, on low for 8 hours.

- Combine the remaining 1 tablespoon butter with the flour, cream, and milk in a small saucepan. Set over medium heat, stirring constantly, until the mixture thickens. Stir the milk mixture into the ingredients in the slow cooker and heat until warmed through. Season with salt and pepper to taste. Remove the bay leaves before serving the chowder.

GLENDA STAECEY
Colville, Washington

"Treat Me Like a Fool" Salmon Stew

Yield: 5 servings

Elvis had a hearty appetite and liked foods that stuck to his ribs. This recipe would work.

1	**pound bacon**	1	**teaspoon seasoning salt**
10	**medium-size red potatoes (skin on or off)**	2	**teaspoons garlic salt**
1	**large onion, chopped**	2	**(6-ounce) cans of salmon, boned and flaked**
2	**teaspoons salt**	4	**cups milk**
1	**teaspoon pepper**	1	**sleeve saltine crackers**

➤ Fry the bacon in a large skillet over medium-high heat until very crisp; drain on paper towels.

➤ Fry the potatoes and onion in a small amount of the bacon grease; then stir in the salt and pepper, seasoning salt, and garlic salt. When the potatoes and onion are tender, add the salmon and mix well.

➤ Add the milk and bring to a simmer (do not boil or the milk will curdle). Simmer for about 15 minutes. Crumble the bacon into the stew; stir well. Serve with saltine crackers.

WENDY A. DYER
Beaufort, South Carolina

Charro's Cowboy Stew

Yield: 4 servings

After watching Elvis in *Charro*, I decided this would be a hearty meal for Elvis the cowboy.

1	**pound ground round**	1	**(16-ounce) can ranch-style beans, with liquid**
1	**(16-ounce) can stewed tomatoes, with liquid**	1	**tablespoon minced garlic**
1	**(16-ounce) can whole-kernel corn, with liquid**		**Salt and pepper**

- Brown the ground round in a Dutch oven over medium heat. Add the tomatoes, corn, beans, garlic, and salt and pepper to taste. Mix well.

- Simmer, covered, for 20 minutes. Serve with cornbread.

BRENDA ROSSER
Wylie, Texas
Official Elvis Insider

"It's Impossible" Vegetable Beef Stew

Yield: 8 servings

3	pounds beef shank, cut in 1-inch cubes	¼	teaspoon chili powder
2	tablespoons vegetable oil	2	bay leaves
6	cups water	1½	cups diced celery
2	cups tomato juice	1½	cups diced carrot
⅓	cup chopped onion	2	cups diced potato
1	tablespoon salt	1	small cabbage, chopped (optional)
2	teaspoons Worcestershire sauce		

- Brown the beef in the oil in a heavy Dutch oven over medium-high heat. Add the water, tomato juice, onion, salt, Worcestershire sauce, chili powder, bay leaves, celery, carrot, potato, and cabbage, if using.

- Simmer, covered, for about 3 hours. Remove the bay leaves to serve.

Cook's Note: You can also add ½ to 1 cup macaroni, if desired.

CARLENE ELVIK
Garden City, South Dakota
Official Elvis Insider

"You Give Me Fever" Gumbo

Yield: 6 to 8 servings

This gumbo has become well known in my community. It is definitely fit for Graceland's table.

4	chicken thighs with skin and bones
2	bay leaves
1	quart water
5	celery stalks, chopped
5	garlic cloves, mashed
¼	cup butter
½	cup vegetable oil
½	cup all-purpose flour
2	green bell peppers, cored, seeded, and chopped
1	to 2 jalapeño peppers, chopped (for less heat, remove the seeds before chopping)
1	large red onion, chopped
1	pound andouille sausage, sliced
1	pound chorizo sausage, sliced
½	teaspoon Louisiana filé powder
2	to 3 teaspoons Creole seasoning
1	pound large uncooked shrimp, peeled and deveined
½	cup chopped scallions
	Salt and pepper

➤ Place the chicken, bay leaves, water, celery, and garlic in a large stockpot. Bring to a boil, lower the heat, and simmer about 45 minutes or until the chicken is tender. Remove the chicken and set it aside to cool. Strain the broth and set it aside to cool.

➤ When the chicken is cool, remove the meat from the bones, discard the bones, and cut the meat into bite-size pieces.

➤ In a large, deep skillet melt the butter and add the oil. Add the flour, stirring over medium-high heat about 10 minutes or until the mixture is a good brown color. Add the green peppers, jalapeño peppers, and onion. Add the andouille and chorizo sausages. Stir until heated through, and then add the filé powder and Creole seasoning.

➤ Pour the sausage mixture into the strained broth and stir to combine. Bring to a boil, reduce the heat, and simmer for about 20 minutes. Add the shrimp and simmer, covered, until the shrimp are pink. Add the chicken, scallions, and salt and pepper to taste.

➤ Serve the gumbo over brown rice with crusty bread. Garnish with additional chopped scallions and a sprinkle of cayenne and Creole seasoning, if desired.

JUDITH MCELWAINE
Port Charlotte, Florida
The Elvis Lovers of South Gulf Cove

An Elvis Memory

I have been an Elvis fan for as long as I can remember—loyal all these years. My Elvis group celebrates his birthday in January and remembers him on August 16 each year with a get-together. I finally visited Graceland not too long ago; it had been a lifelong dream.

"King Creole" Shrimp Creole

Yield: 4 to 6 servings

I don't know if Elvis was a seafood lover, but I do know that if he were sitting at my kitchen table right now, this mouth-watering dish would get his taste buds "all shook up." Just the spices alone would have him saying, "All right," and after giving an award-winning performance by eating a second helping, he would be back at Graceland with precious thoughts of a night well spent and a warm feeling all the way down to his blue suede shoes

3	pounds uncooked medium shrimp, peeled and deveined
¼	teaspoon parsley
¼	teaspoon thyme
1	bay leaf
2	whole cloves
1	garlic clove
¼	cup bacon fat or vegetable oil
1	cup finely chopped onion
¾	cup finely chopped celery
¾	cup cored, seeded, and finely chopped green bell pepper
3	(14.5-ounce) cans stewed tomatoes, with liquid
¼	teaspoon chili powder
½	teaspoon salt
¼	teaspoon pepper
¼	teaspoon celery seed
¼	teaspoon cayenne (or to taste)
	Hot cooked rice

➤ Bring a large pot of water to a boil. Add the shrimp and cook just until they turn pink. Remove the shrimp from the water. Reserve 2 cups of the cooking water.

➤ Wrap the parsley, thyme, bay leaf, cloves, and garlic in a small piece of cheesecloth as an herb bouquet garni.

➤ Melt the bacon fat in a large skillet over medium heat and sauté the onion, celery, and green pepper until translucent but not brown. Add the tomatoes with their liquid, the chili powder, salt, pepper, celery seed, cayenne, reserved cooking water, and the herb bouquet garni.

➤ Simmer, covered, for 40 minutes, occasionally mashing the tomatoes and stirring with a wooden spoon. Add the shrimp to the sauce and simmer 8 minutes. Serve over rice.

GARLENE DELEKTA
Sterling Heights, Michigan
Founding member, Official Elvis Insider

Did You Know?

Elvis made his network television debut in 1956 on the CBS variety show, "Stage Show," hosted by Tommy and Jimmy Dorsey. He sang a "Shake, Rattle, and Roll" and "Flip, Flop, and Fly" medley and "I Got a Woman."

A True Elvis Story

In early 1971 Elvis, a few of his friends, and I decided to go to Tupelo for the afternoon. The main purpose was to visit the Lee County Sheriff, who was a former classmate of mine, to obtain a special deputy commission for Elvis.

"While in Tupelo, we drove to Old Saltillo Road, where Elvis had lived and which was just a short distance from my grandmother's house. I told Elvis that she was quite ill, and he decided we should pay her a visit.

"Typical of Elvis's compassion, he affectionately addressed her as "Maw," which was what she was called by her grandchildren. We had a great visit, and later that evening, after we'd returned to Memphis, my aunt called my mother to tell her how excited Maw had been to see Elvis, but that she was curious to know who was the other fellow with him.

"Elvis really got a kick out of Maw's not recognizing her own grandson, but, personally, I think she was just 'all shook up.'"

BILL MORRIS
Memphis, Tennessee
Mayor of Shelby County from 1978 to 1994

Elvis never forgot the humble beginnings of his birthplace in Tupelo, Mississippi.

Eight

Desserts

Graceland's Table

"Can't Help Falling in Love" German Chocolate Upside-Down Cake

"Devil in Disguise" Chocolate-Filled Cupcakes

Trouble Chocolate Éclairs

"Too Much" Chocolate Cake

"Treat Me Nice" Cherry Cake

"Today, Tomorrow, and Forever" Peanut Butter Cake

"That's All Right" Carrot Cake

"You're So . . ." Square Cake

"Paradise, Hawaiian Style" Piña Colada Cake

Banana Cake

Chocolate "Angel in Disguise" Cake with Filling

Janelle McComb's Whipped Cream Pound Cake

"For the Good Times" Punch Bowl Cake

Cranberry Pudding

"Loving You" Strawberry Crisp

"If I Can Dream" Pie

"Aloha from Hawaii" Cheesecake

"Impossible Dream" Cherry Pie

Hunk O' Peanut Butter Pie

Pecan Pie

"Can't Help Falling in Love" with Southern Pecan Pie

Egg Pie

"Just Pretend" Pecan Pie

"American Trilogy" Apple Pie

"Frankie and Johnny" Apple Tart

"Cindy, Cindy" Pineapple Fried Pies

Scatter Chunky Monkey Parfaits

The Wonder of Your Crêpes

"Mess of Blues" Pecan Bars

"A Little Less Conversation" Bars

"Merry Christmas, Baby" Berry Bars

"It's Now or Never" Brownies with Fudge Topping

Old-Fashioned Sugar Cookies

Texas Cow Patties

Hunka Hunka Chocolate Chip Macadamia Cookies

"Promised Land" Cookies

"If I Can Dream" Heavenly Cookies

"Heartbreak Hotel" Peanut Butter Drops

Marian Cocke's Banana Pudding

"TCB" Ice Cream Delight

"Double Trouble" Trifle

Banana Pudding

Blue Hawaiian Pineapple

Bossa Nova Bread-and-Butter Pudding

"Loving You" Pecan-Raisin Bread Pudding

"Tutti Frutti" Raspberry Divinity

Peanut Butter and Nanner Goo Balls

Peanut Butter Fudge

"Crying in the Chapel" Stained Glass Windows

"Can't Help Falling in Love" German Chocolate Upside-Down Cake

Yield: 12 servings

You'll fall in love with this cake once you take the first bite. I think Elvis would too.

1½	**cups shredded coconut**
1½	**cups chopped pecans**
1	**(18.25-ounce) box German chocolate cake mix**
½	**cup (1 stick) butter or margarine**
1	**(8-ounce) package cream cheese, softened**
1	**(16-ounce) box confectioners' sugar**

- Preheat the oven to 350 degrees. Grease a 9 x 13-inch baking dish.

- Spread the coconut and pecans in the bottom of the prepared baking dish. Prepare the cake mix batter as directed on the package. Pour over the coconut and pecans.

- Heat the butter, cream cheese, and confectioners' sugar in a medium saucepan over medium-low heat and mix well. Pour over the cake batter.

- Bake for 40 to 45 minutes. Remove from the oven and cool on a wire rack before serving.

Cook's Note: Serve with whipped topping, if desired.

CATHY WAGGONER
Webb City, Missouri
Return to Sender Club

"Devil in Disguise"
Chocolate-Filled Cupcakes

Yield: 24 cupcakes

Elvis loved peanut butter, so using the peanut butter chips would have pleased him. Chocolate and peanut butter . . . yum!

1	(18.25-ounce) package chocolate cake mix
1	(8-ounce) package cream cheese, softened
⅓	cup sugar
1	large egg
	Dash of salt
1	(6-ounce) package chocolate or peanut butter chips
24	cupcake papers

➤ Preheat the oven to 350 degrees.

➤ Prepare the cake mix batter according to package directions.

➤ Combine the cream cheese, sugar, egg, and salt in a small bowl and mix well. Stir in the chocolate or peanut butter chips. Place the cupcake papers in the muffin tin cups. Fill the cups half full of cake batter. Spoon about 1 teaspoon of the cream cheese mixture onto each half cup of cake batter; fill the cups with additional batter.

➤ Bake for about 20 minutes or until a toothpick inserted in the center of a cupcake comes out clean. Frost if desired.

MARY B. SETTLE
Assaria, Kansas
Founding member, Official Elvis Insider

Trouble Chocolate Éclairs

Yield: 15 to 18 éclairs

This dessert is so delicious that it's fit for a "king." I think Elvis would have loved it, and it's so rich that one panfull would have been enough to serve all the company he had at Graceland.

2	**(6-ounce) boxes vanilla pudding**
2	**cups cold milk**
2	**(8-ounce) containers frozen whipped topping, thawed**
1	**(16-ounce) box graham crackers**
1	**(16-ounce) container chocolate fudge frosting**
2	**tablespoons hot water**

➤ Empty both boxes of pudding into a large mixing bowl. Add the cold milk and mix well. Stir in both containers of whipped topping. Line the bottom of a 9 x 13-inch baking pan with one-third of the whole graham crackers, breaking off smaller pieces to fit in the corners.

➤ Spread with half the pudding mixture. Layer with one-third more of the graham crackers, then the remaining pudding mixture. Top with the remaining graham crackers.

➤ Put the frosting in a medium bowl, add the hot water, and stir well. Pour the frosting over the top layer of graham crackers and spread it to the edges of the pan.

➤ Chill at least 4 hours or overnight. Cut into squares to serve.

GAYLE BELLOMY
Union, Ohio

"Too Much" Chocolate Cake

Yield: 12 servings

This cake takes only an hour from start to finish—a good recipe to have handy. You can also freeze it for use at a later time.

2	cups all-purpose flour
2	cups sugar
1	teaspoon baking soda
1	teaspoon ground cinnamon
1	cup (2 sticks) butter
1	cup water
¼	cup unsweetened cocoa powder
½	cup plain yogurt
2	large eggs
1	teaspoon vanilla extract

CHOCOLATE ICING

6	tablespoons butter
¼	cup unsweetened cocoa powder
⅓	cup plain yogurt
2½	cups confectioners' sugar, sifted
1	teaspoon vanilla extract
1	cup chopped walnuts

➤ Preheat the oven to 350 degrees. Grease and flour a 15½ x 10½ x 1-inch jellyroll pan.

➤ In a large bowl combine the flour, sugar, baking soda, and cinnamon. Bring the butter, water, and cocoa to a boil in a medium saucepan over high heat, and pour the hot mixture over the dry ingredients. Beat at medium speed until well combined, scraping the sides of the bowl occasionally. Add the yogurt, eggs, and vanilla, and continue beating just until mixed. Pour the batter into the prepared pan and bake for 15 to 20 minutes or until a toothpick inserted in the center comes out clean. Do not overcook; the cake should be very moist. Remove the cake from the oven and cool on a wire rack for 5 to 10 minutes.

➤ For the icing, combine the butter, cocoa, and yogurt in a medium saucepan; bring to a rapid boil over high heat, stirring constantly, and then remove from the heat. Stir in the confectioners' sugar and vanilla until smooth. Place dollops of Chocolate Icing on the warm cake to melt and then spread to the edges. Sprinkle with the chopped nuts.

➤ Serve immediately or cover and freeze for up to four weeks. Thaw, unwrapped, at room temperature about 2 to 3 hours before serving.

DEBORAH A. CROSSON
New Port Richey, Florida

"Treat Me Nice" Cherry Cake

Yield: 20 servings

My Gran passed this recipe to my mom. It's a rich dessert that's usually made over the holidays. I think Elvis might have given up his banana pudding for this sweet cake.

1	cup (2 sticks) butter
1½	cups sugar
4	large eggs
1	teaspoon pure vanilla extract
1	teaspoon almond extract
2	cups all-purpose flour
1	(16-ounce) can cherry pie filling
	Confectioners' sugar

➤ Preheat the oven to 350 degrees. Grease a 15 x 10-inch baking pan.

➤ Cream the butter slowly in a large bowl. Add the sugar and beat until fluffy. Add the eggs, one at a time, beating well after each addition. Add the extracts and the flour, stirring well. Pour the batter into the prepared pan. With a butter knife, cut the batter in the pan into 20 squares. Add about a teaspoon of the pie filling to each square.

➤ Bake for 35 to 40 minutes. Remove from the oven and sift confectioners' sugar over the warm cake.

NADINE SLIWA
Chicago, Illinois
Illinois Fan Club

I Was at Graceland the Day Elvis Died

My mother was an enormous Elvis fan. She was born in 1944, and her family got its first television in 1956, when she was twelve, so one of the first things she saw on television was Elvis on the *Ed Sullivan Show*.

"When I was a little girl, we were living in Oxford, Mississippi. My mother had gone back to school to complete her master's degree as a reading specialist, and right after she graduated, we went on a family vacation to Hot Springs, Arkansas. We were there one morning, sweating in the diamond mines. No one ever finds anything in those diamond mines anyway, so eventually we left and went into a little shop where they sold taffy made with water from the springs. We looked pretty hot and scraggly, and there was a man standing there who seemed to me to be about a hundred years old—remember, I was nine at the time. The radio was on, playing Elvis songs, with people breaking in and talking every once in a while. Finally, my mother asked the man what was happening, what were they talking about.

"He said, 'Don't you know, Honey? Elvis died today,' in what seemed to me a really creepy voice.

"Well, my mother just lost her mind. Within fifteen minutes of his saying that, we were packed and in the car driving to Memphis. Now you have to remember, this was my mother. She'd just gotten her master's. She was a pretty serious woman, so this was a side of her I'd never seen before.

"I'd already been to Graceland. When we moved to Oxford, we'd made the trip to Tupelo to see 'the birthplace,' and then we'd gone to Memphis. Lisa Marie was about my age; and once when we went to Graceland, she was there swimming in the pool, so I had felt like I'd met Elvis and his family. But on this day it was a mob scene. It was August 16, so it was terribly hot—probably about 110 degrees. People were trying to jump the walls. People were passing out and getting crushed trying to squeeze through the gates, and there were ambulances all over the place waiting to take them away.

"My mother just kept crying and repeating, 'I never got to see him in concert.' I had no idea what I was doing there, and I was absolutely scared to death. I actually had dreams about it for weeks.

"I think there are a couple of reasons why it had such an impact on me. First of all, this was really the first time I realized my mother wasn't just a mom. She liked rock and roll; she had actually been a teenager at some point. And the second thing was that this was my first experience with death. In fact, when I got to college and took a course on the sociology of death and grieving, we were asked to write about our first experience of death, and I wrote about that day.

"My mother is still a great Elvis fan, and she has quite a collection of 'stuff,' including a huge, eighty-pound, wooden disk with a painting of a very Hispanic-looking Elvis on it that she found in a hotel when she and my father were on vacation in Belize. It was done by the wife of the hotel owner, and he gave it to her when she left, so it's now hanging on the wall of their home in Mississippi.

"And I guess it did rub off, because I'm quite a fan myself. I have a charm bracelet with pictures of Elvis from birth to death that I bought in a little shop in Memphis. And now that I'm living in Tupelo, I find myself venturing to the birthplace for celebrations. I went to the fan appreciation day they have every August with a concert and food, and I bought myself a lunchbox in the gift shop. It's right down the street from where I live, so I can just pop by, but that day there was an incredibly diverse group of tourists who had come a long distance, including three busloads of British and German fans. And if you go to Graceland any weekday afternoon, you can see cars from all over the country and hear accents from all over the world.

"It's been almost thirty years since that day in Hot Springs when we found out Elvis had died, but it seems like he's got even more people loving him now."

DEBBY WEST
Tupelo, Mississippi

"Today, Tomorrow, and Forever" Peanut Butter Cake

Yield: 12 to 20 servings

You know Elvis and peanut butter. He would have loved this cake.

- ½ cup smooth peanut butter
- 1 cup water
- 1 cup (2 sticks) butter or margarine
- 2 cups all-purpose flour
- 2 cups sugar
- 1 teaspoon salt
- 1 teaspoon baking soda
- 2 large eggs
- ½ cup buttermilk

PEANUT BUTTER FROSTING
- ½ cup (1 stick) butter or margarine
- ¼ cup peanut butter
- 3 tablespoons buttermilk
- ½ teaspoon vanilla extract
- 2 cups confectioners' sugar

➤ Preheat the oven to 350 degrees. Grease a 13 x 9-inch baking pan.

➤ Combine the peanut butter, water, and butter in a medium saucepan and bring to a rapid boil over high heat. Combine the flour, sugar, salt, and baking soda in a large bowl. Pour the hot peanut butter mixture over the dry ingredients and mix well. Stir in the eggs and buttermilk.

➤ Pour the batter into the prepared pan and bake for 35 to 40 minutes.

➤ Prepare the frosting. Combine the butter, peanut butter, and buttermilk in a medium saucepan and bring to a rapid boil over high heat. Stir in the vanilla and confectioners' sugar.

➤ Remove the cake from the oven and spread the frosting on top while the cake is still warm.

GINGER JOHNSON
Williamston, Michigan

"That's All Right" Carrot Cake

Yield: 12 servings

I believe this is just the type of cake Elvis's mama, Gladys, would have made for him to enjoy at Graceland's dinner table.

2	**cups all-purpose flour**
2	**cups sugar**
1	**teaspoon baking powder**
1	**teaspoon baking soda**
1	**teaspoon ground cinnamon**
1½	**cups vegetable oil**
4	**large eggs**
3	**cups (about 1 pound) grated carrots**

CREAM CHEESE FROSTING

1	**(8-ounce) package cream cheese, softened**
1	**pound confectioners' sugar**
2	**teaspoons vanilla extract**
1	**cup shredded coconut (optional)**
½	**cup chopped nuts of your choice (optional)**
½	**cup (1 stick) butter or margarine, softened**

➤ Preheat the oven to 325 degrees. Grease and flour a 13 x 9-inch baking pan.

➤ Combine the flour, sugar, baking powder, baking soda, and cinnamon in a large bowl. Add the vegetable oil and eggs and blend well. Stir in the grated carrots. Pour the cake mixture into the prepared pan and bake for 45 minutes or until a toothpick inserted in the center comes out clean.

➤ While the cake is baking, prepare the frosting. Combine the cream cheese, sugar, vanilla, coconut and nuts if using, and the butter in a medium bowl until smooth. When the cake is cool frost it with the Cream Cheese Frosting. Keep refrigerated until ready to serve.

JACQUELYN D. DEMARCO
Holley, New York
Official Elvis Insider

"You're So . . ." Square Cake

Yield: 12 to 15 servings

Elvis loved desserts, even before he could walk. He would have loved this recipe, which is really fit for a king.

1	(18-ounce) box yellow cake mix
½	cup (1 stick) butter, melted
3	plus 2 large eggs
1	(16-ounce) box confectioners' sugar
1	(12-ounce) tub soft cream cheese

➤ Preheat the oven to 350 degrees. Lightly grease a 9 x 12-inch baking pan.

➤ Combine the cake mix, butter, and 2 eggs in a large bowl; mix well. Pat the mixture into the prepared baking pan.

➤ In a medium bowl beat together the confectioners' sugar, cream cheese, and the remaining 3 eggs. Pour the sugar mixture over the cake mixture.

➤ Bake for 40 minutes; let cool completely. Cut into squares to serve.

EARL GREEN
Jacksonville, Florida

"Paradise, Hawaiian Style" Piña Colada Cake

Yield: 6 to 8 servings

1	(15-ounce) package yellow cake mix
1	(8-ounce) can cream of coconut
1	(12-ounce) can sweetened condensed milk
1	(20-ounce) can crushed pineapple, drained
1	(8-ounce) container frozen whipped topping, thawed

- Prepare the cake batter according to package directions and bake in a 9 x 13-inch baking pan.

- Combine the cream of coconut and condensed milk in a small bowl. Punch holes in the cake and pour the mixture over the top. Spread the pineapple over the top of the cake. Cover with the whipped topping.

- Refrigerate for at least 1 hour before serving.

Cook's Note: Possible variations include adding rum flavoring to the cake batter and toasted coconut to the whipped topping.

MARLENE NUNEZ
Violet, Louisiana
Elvis Country Fan Club

Banana Cake

Yield: 10 servings

This recipe has passed from generation to generation in our family and is always made with love. Elvis would have enjoyed it as much as we do.

8	tablespoons (1 stick) butter or margarine	1¼	cups sugar
2	large eggs	2	cups all-purpose flour
2	ripe bananas, mashed	½	teaspoon salt
1	teaspoon vanilla extract	1	teaspoon baking powder
½	cup sour milk (½ cup milk and 1 teaspoon vinegar)	1	teaspoon baking soda

- Preheat the oven to 350 degrees. Grease and flour a 9 x 13-inch baking pan.

- Combine the butter, eggs, bananas, vanilla, sour milk, and sugar in a large bowl; mix well. Combine the flour, salt, baking powder, and baking soda in a medium bowl; mix well with a fork. Stir the dry ingredients into the liquid mixture and mix well.

- Pour the cake mixture into the prepared pan and bake for 30 to 35 minutes or until a toothpick inserted in the center comes out clean.

TERRI ZEZZA
Exeter, Pennsylvania

Chocolate "Angel in Disguise" Cake with Filling

Yield: 10 to 12 servings

This recipe was given to me by my grandmother.

1½	cups plus 2 tablespoons sugar
½	cup unsweetened cocoa powder
1	cup cake flour
¼	teaspoon salt
12	large egg whites
2	teaspoons vanilla extract
1½	teaspoons cream of tartar

CUSTARD FILLING

3	large eggs
⅓	cup sugar
	Dash of salt
2	cups milk or half-and-half
1	teaspoon vanilla extract
1	pint whipping cream, whipped

➤ Preheat the oven to 375 degrees.

➤ Sift the sugar and cocoa together six or seven times in a medium bowl. Mix in the flour. Combine the salt, egg whites, and vanilla in a large mixing bowl and beat until foamy. Add the cream of tartar and beat the egg whites until stiff but not dry. Slowly fold in the sugar mixture by hand, adding it a little at a time until it disappears into the egg whites.

➤ Pour the mixture into an ungreased, 10-inch, tube pan. Gently cut through the batter with a spatula to break up any air bubbles.

➤ Bake for 30 to 35 minutes or until the top springs back when touched lightly with your finger, or when cracks in the top feel dry to the touch.

➤ While the cake is baking prepare the filling. Combine the eggs, sugar, and salt in the top of a double boiler over hot, not boiling, water. Do not let the top pan touch the water. Gradually whisk in the milk and cook over medium heat, stirring constantly, about 20 minutes or until the custard is very thick. Remove from the heat and stir in the vanilla. Pour the custard into a medium bowl. Refrigerate until firm, and then fold the whipped cream into the cooled custard.

➤ When the cake is done invert the tube pan on a funnel or a bottle and let it hang until the cake has cooled completely. Remove the cake from the pan. With a serrated knife, using a gentle, sawing motion, cut the top off the cake and add a layer of the custard filling. Replace the top and frost the entire cake with the remaining filling.

ANNA HAMILTON
Bartlett, Tennessee

An Elvis Memory

I attended Humes High School, the same one Elvis attended, and consider him my hero. I own and operate Anna's Steakhouse and have my personal Elvis collection proudly displayed there as well as a Humes Room, which is filled with memorabilia from our alma mater.

The Dream Did Come True

From the two-room house in Tupelo, Mississippi, where Elvis was born, it is only one hundred miles as the crow flies to Graceland, where he died."

"Elvis always told his parents he was going to grow up and buy them a great big house. "The dream did come true, and it was a dream just to be able to take a peek inside the mansion. I was one of the friends who was able to walk its entirety, always amazed by Elvis's humble attitude as he proudly took me, and perhaps a friend, on a personal tour. One night my beautiful niece, Robin, then age twelve, accompanied me to Graceland. After taking us around, even into

"Robin" with Elvis.   Courtesy of Janelle McComb

the trophy room especially to let Robin look at his collection, we were back in the foyer when Elvis put his arm around Robin and asked, 'Robin, who is your favorite singer?'

She immediately said, 'Donny Osmond,' who was just then breaking on the musical scene with his brothers and sisters.

"Elvis laughed and looked at Robin, and said, 'You are in my house and you tell me that Donny Osmond is your favorite singer?'

"With all the honesty instilled in her by her loving parents,

Robin looked up and said, 'But, Elvis, you wanted me to tell you the truth, didn't you? Besides, you're too old for me.'

"Again, he put his arm around her and said, 'Robin, stay as precious and honest as you are today and the world will be a better place to live.' "

JANELLE MCCOMB
Tupelo, Mississippi

The recipe for that cake, which often found its way into Graceland's kitchen, follows.

Janelle McComb's Whipped Cream Pound Cake

Yield: 12 to 15 servings

3 cups sugar	**3** cups cake flour, sifted twice, divided
1 stick (8 tablespoons) butter, softened	**1** cup whipping cream
7 eggs, at room temperature	**2** teaspoons vanilla extract

➤ Butter and flour a 10-inch tube pan.

➤ Cream the sugar and butter together in a large bowl. Add the eggs, one at a time, beating well after each addition. Mix in half the flour, then the whipping cream, then the remaining flour. Stir in the vanilla.

➤ Pour the batter into the prepared pan and set it in a cold oven. Turn the heat to 350 degrees and bake for 60 to 70 minutes or until a sharp knife inserted in the cake comes out clean. Cool in the pan for 5 minutes; then remove the cake and cool completely.

Cook's Note: Well wrapped, the cake will keep for several days.

JANELLE MCCOMB
Tupelo, Mississippi

"For the Good Times"
Punch Bowl Cake

Yield: 8 servings

1	(15-ounce) package white or yellow cake mix
6	to 8 ripe bananas, sliced, divided in thirds
1	plus 1 (12-ounce) cans blueberry pie filling
1	(16-ounce) container frozen whipped topping, thawed, divided
1	plus 1 (12-ounce) cans cherry or strawberry pie filling
1	(20-ounce) can crushed pineapple, drained
½	cup coconut flakes
½	cup chopped pecans
½	cup chocolate syrup

➤ Prepare and bake the cake according to the package directions.

➤ Cut the cake in quarters and crumble one of the quarters in the bottom of a punch bowl. Layer with one-third of the bananas, 1 can blueberry pie filling, and one-fourth of the whipped topping. Repeat the layering with a second quarter of the cake crumbled, one-third of the bananas, 1 can cherry pie filling, and one-fourth of the whipped topping. For the third layering, use a third crumbled cake quarter, the remaining one-third of the bananas, the remaining can of blueberry pie filling, and one-fourth of the topping. Crumble the final quarter of the cake on top, followed by the remaining can of cherry pie filling, the pineapple, and the remaining one-fourth of the whipped topping.

➤ Garnish with the coconut, pecans, and chocolate syrup.

MARLENE NUNEZ
Violet, Louisiana
Elvis Country Fan Club

Cranberry Pudding

Yield: 6 to 8 servings

½   **cup sugar**

1½   **tablespoons butter**

½   **cup milk**

1   **cup all-purpose flour**

1½   **teaspoons baking powder**

1½   **to 2 cups whole cranberries, washed**

VANILLA SAUCE

1   **cup sugar**

1   **cup (2 sticks) butter**

½   **cup cream**

1   **teaspoon vanilla extract**

➤ Preheat the oven to 400 degrees. Lightly grease and flour an 8-inch cake pan.

➤ Cream the sugar and butter together in a medium bowl. Stir in the milk, flour, and baking powder. Fold in the cranberries. Pour into the prepared pan and bake 30 to 45 minutes or until a toothpick inserted in the center comes out clean.

➤ While the cake is baking prepare the vanilla sauce. Combine the sugar, butter, cream, and vanilla in a saucepan and cook over medium heat, stirring constantly, until slightly thickened. Serve the cake warm with the sauce.

PATTI CARPENTER
Irvine, California

"Loving You" Strawberry Crisp

Yield: 9 to 12 servings

1½	**cups all-purpose flour**
½	**cup chopped pecans**
½	**cup (1 stick) butter melted**
2	**(3-ounce) packages cream cheese, softened**
¾	**can sweetened condensed milk**
1	**(6-ounce) package strawberry glaze**
1	**quart sliced strawberries**

➤ Preheat the oven to 350 degrees. Lightly grease a 9 x 13-inch baking pan.

➤ Combine the flour, pecans, and butter in a medium bowl and mix well. Pat into the bottom of the prepared pan and bake for 10 minutes. Remove from the oven and cool on a wire rack.

➤ Combine the cream cheese and milk in a small bowl and mix well. If the mixture is not thick enough, add some confectioners' sugar to thicken. Spread over the cooled crust. Prepare the glaze according to the package directions. Combine with the strawberries and spread over the cream cheese mixture.

➤ Refrigerate the dessert until ready to serve, and then cut it into squares.

NANCY WYMER
Sikeston, Missouri

"If I Can Dream" Pie

Yield: 6 to 8 servings

'If I Can Dream.' I would love to have made this pie in Graceland's kitchen and to have served it to Elvis.

40	**large marshmallows**
12	**(0.5 ounce) chocolate candy bars, crushed, or 6 ounces semisweet chocolate morsels**
1	**cup milk**
2	**cups frozen whipped topping, thawed**
1	**(10-inch) prepared graham cracker piecrust**
	Graham cracker crumbs

➢ Combine the marshmallows, crushed candy, and milk in a microwave-safe dish. Microwave on low for 30 seconds. Stir and continue to microwave on low for an additional 30 seconds until melted; stir well.

➢ Cool and then fold in the whipped topping. Pour the mixture into the piecrust and sprinkle with the graham cracker crumbs. Chill and serve cold.

Cook's Note: Add a dollop of whipped cream to each serving, if desired.

BECKE AMMONS
Fort Worth, Indiana
Official Elvis Insider

"Aloha from Hawaii" Cheesecake

Yield: 8 to 10 servings

This cheesecake, which is made with gelatin, is light enough to melt in your mouth.

1	**(3-ounce) package island pineapple gelatin**
1	**cup boiling water**
½	**cup (1 stick) butter, melted**
1½	**cups graham cracker crumbs**
1	**plus ¼ cup sugar**
1	**(8-ounce) package cream cheese, softened**
1	**(8-ounce) can evaporated milk, chilled**
2	**teaspoons vanilla extract**

➤ Combine the gelatin with the boiling water and stir until the gelatin is dissolved. In a small bowl combine the butter with the graham cracker crumbs and ¼ cup sugar; mix well. Press three-fourths of the mixture into the bottom of a 9 x 9-inch glass dish.

➤ Using an electric mixer, combine the cream cheese and the remaining 1 cup sugar in a medium bowl. In a large bowl whip the evaporated milk with the vanilla until smooth and creamy. Add the cooled gelatin and the cream cheese mixture and mix well.

➤ Pour over the prepared crust and sprinkle with the remaining one-fourth of the graham cracker crumb mixture. Chill at least 6 hours or overnight.

Cook's Note: Use green or red gelatin for the holidays.

ELAINE SMITYH
Aurora, Illinois

"Impossible Dream" Cherry Pie

Yield: 8 servings

If you love cherry pie, you will love this treat.

¾	**cup milk**
2	**tablespoons butter or margarine**
½	**teaspoon almond extract**
2	**large eggs**
½	**cup baking mix (such as Bisquick)**
¼	**cup sugar**
1	**(16-ounce) can cherry pie filling**

STREUSEL TOPPING

2	**tablespoons butter or margarine**
½	**cup baking mix (such as Bisquick)**
½	**cup packed dark brown sugar**
½	**teaspoon ground cinnamon**

➤ Preheat the oven to 400 degrees. Grease a 9-inch pie plate.

➤ Beat together the milk, butter, almond extract, eggs, baking mix, and sugar in a medium bowl. Pour the mixture into the prepared pie plate. Spoon the pie filling evenly over the top. Bake for 25 to 35 minutes.

➤ While the pie is baking prepare the topping. Combine the butter, baking mix, brown sugar, and cinnamon in a small bowl until crumbly. Spoon on the Streusel Topping and bake a few minutes longer, until the topping is browned. Serve warm; refrigerate leftovers.

Cook's Note: Serve with ice cream or whipped topping, if you wish.

CATHY WAGGONER
Webb City, Missouri
Return to Sender Club

Hunk O' Peanut Butter Pie

Yield: 8 servings

If I'd had this peanut butter pie recipe years ago, I would have baked it for Elvis. It has become a holiday favorite for my family.

1	(9-inch) deep-dish pie shell
1	cup confectioners' sugar
½	cup smooth peanut butter
2	cups milk
2	tablespoons butter
¼	teaspoon salt
⅔	cup plus 3 tablespoons granulated sugar
¼	cup cornstarch
3	large eggs, separated
¼	teaspoon vanilla extract
	Cream of tartar

➤ Preheat the oven to 375 degrees. Bake the piecrust until it browns lightly, about 13 minutes.

➤ Using a pastry cutter, combine the confectioners' sugar and peanut butter in a large bowl until the mixture is very fine and crumbly. Evenly spread three-fourths of the mixture into the pie shell.

➤ Combine the milk, butter, and salt in a medium saucepan over medium-high heat. Scald or heat the mixture until it begins to bubble, and then remove from the heat.

➤ Mix ⅔ cup granulated sugar and the cornstarch in a medium bowl. Blend in the egg yolks, one at a time, stirring rapidly with a whisk until the mixture is smooth. Add the egg mixture to the hot milk, return the pan to the heat, and, stirring constantly to prevent scorching, heat until the mixture is thickened. Remove from the heat and stir in the vanilla extract. Pour into the pie shell.

➤ Beat the egg whites in a large bowl. Add the remaining 3 tablespoons sugar and small amounts of cream of tartar as needed to help the egg whites come to stiff peaks. Spread the meringue on top of the pie and seal to the edges. Sprinkle the remaining one-fourth of the peanut butter mixture on top of the meringue.

➤ Bake for about 15 minutes or until the meringue is slightly brown. Cool the pie and then refrigerate. Serve cold.

Cook's Notes: To help the egg whites form stiff peaks, begin with eggs that are at room temperature. To give your pie a professional appearance, use a butter knife or spoon to gently swirl the meringue into small peaks before baking.

BELINDA BRYANT
Montgomery, Alabama

FROM ELVIS'S KITCHEN

Pecan Pie

Yield: 6 to 8 servings

½	cup (1 stick) butter, melted
4	large eggs
2	tablespoons all-purpose flour
1	cup light corn syrup
1	teaspoon salt
1	cup sugar
1	cup water
1½	cups chopped pecans
1	(9-inch) unbaked pie shell

➤ Preheat the oven to 325 degrees.

➤ Combine the melted butter, eggs, flour, corn syrup, salt, sugar, and water in a large bowl; mix well. Fold in the pecans. Pour into the pie shell and bake for about 1 hour or until the center is set.

"Can't Help Falling in Love" with Southern Pecan Pie

Yield: 6 to 8 servings

Elvis, with his sweet tooth, would have loved this recipe, as would any king.

1 cup packed dark brown sugar	½ cup (1 stick) butter, melted
½ cup granulated sugar	1 cup pecan halves
1 tablespoon all-purpose flour	1 (9-inch) deep-dish pie shell
2 large eggs	Frozen whipped topping, thawed (optional)
2 tablespoons milk	
1 teaspoon vanilla extract	

➤ Preheat the oven to 350 degrees.

➤ Combine both sugars and the flour in a large bowl. Beat the eggs and milk in a medium bowl, stir in the vanilla, and pour into the sugar mixture. Add the butter, mixing well. Fold in the nuts.

➤ Pour the filling mixture into the pie shell and bake for 40 to 50 minutes or until the center is set. Serve slightly warm, with whipped topping if desired.

CAROL FRANKS
Smyrna, Tennessee

FROM ELVIS'S KITCHEN

Egg Pie

Yield: 6 to 8 servings

4 large eggs	1 tablespoon vanilla extract
1½ cups sugar	1½ sticks butter
1 tablespoon cornstarch	1 pinch of salt
3 cups milk or cream	1 (9-inch) unbaked pie shell

- Preheat the oven to 300 degrees.

- Beat the eggs in a medium bowl; add the sugar, cornstarch, milk, vanilla, butter, and salt. Mix well and pour into the pie shell. Place in the oven and bake for 40 to 50 minutes or until the pie is set in the middle.

"Just Pretend" Pecan Pie

Yield: 8 servings

Pecan pie is a staple in the South, always appreciated and enjoyed by true southerners. Elvis was certainly a true southerner in every sense of the word.

1	cup dark corn syrup	1	teaspoon vanilla extract
¾	cup sugar	1	cup chopped pecans
3	large eggs, lightly beaten	1	(9-inch) pie shell
3	tablespoons butter		

- Preheat the oven to 350 degrees.

- Combine the corn syrup and sugar in a medium saucepan, bring to a boil over high heat, and boil for 2 minutes.

- Pour the mixture slowly over the beaten eggs in a medium bowl. Continue stirring, and add the butter, vanilla, and pecans. Pour the filling into the pie shell and bake for 35 to 40 minutes or until set.

LISA R. STEWART
Madison, Tennessee
If I Can Dream Elvis Fan Club, Washington State
(In memory of my great-grandmother Bettie F. Elrod)

"American Trilogy" Apple Pie

Yield: 6 to 8 servings

I understand that apple pie was one of Elvis's favorite desserts and his mother, Gladys, fixed it often. This third-generation recipe is a tribute to a Presley favorite.

CRUMB TOPPING

1½	cups all-purpose flour
1	cup sugar
1	cup butter or margarine

PIE FILLING

¾	cup sugar
¼	cup all-purpose flour
½	teaspoon nutmeg

½	teaspoon ground cloves
½	teaspoon ground cinnamon
	Dash of salt
6	cups peeled, sliced tart apples, such as Rome
1	tablespoon tapioca beads
1	(9-inch) deep-dish pie shell
2	tablespoons butter or margarine

➤ Preheat the oven to 425 degrees.

➤ For the topping, combine the flour and sugar in a small bowl. Work in the butter with your finger tips until the mixture is crumbly.

➤ For the filling stir together the sugar, flour, nutmeg, cloves, cinnamon, and salt in a large bowl; mix well. Mix in the apples and tapioca beads.

➤ Spoon the filling into the pie shell and cover loosely with the topping. Dot with the butter and bake for 40 to 50 minutes. Cover the pie with foil after 25 minutes or the topping will burn

Cook's Note: Serve with cinnamon or maple ice cream.

JULIE ANN LAWRENCE
Gladstone, Oklahoma

"Frankie and Johnny" Apple Tart

Yield: 6 servings

Elvis loved this land from sea to shining sea. And since apples are as American as any food can be, I blended some spices and mixed just the right things, promising an aroma and taste truly fit for the King.

3	cups all-purpose flour	6	to 8 Granny Smith apples, cored and sliced
2	cups plus 4 tablespoons butter, softened	2	teaspoons vanilla extract
1¼	plus ½ cups sugar	2	tablespoons lemon juice
		1	teaspoon ground cinnamon

➤ Preheat the oven to 350 degrees.

➤ Combine the flour, 2 cups butter, and 1¼ cups sugar in a large bowl; mix with a pastry cutter until crumbly.

➤ Combine the apples, the remaining ½ cup sugar, the vanilla, lemon juice, and cinnamon in a medium bowl. Melt the remaining 4 tablespoons butter and add to the apple mixture; mix well.

➤ Press the crust into a tart pan or pie plate and trim the edges, reserving the leftover dough. Spoon the apple mixture into the crust. Crumble the leftover dough and sprinkle it over the filling.

➤ Bake for 45 minutes or until the top is well browned.

SHANNON PELLETIER SWANSON
Apopka, Florida

"Cindy, Cindy" Pineapple Fried Pies

Yield: 6 to 8 servings

I remember Elvis in *Blue Hawaii*. How beautiful and handsome he was then—and always will be. Elvis would love this recipe just because it tastes so good.

1	(8-ounce) can crushed pineapple		6	to 8 flour tortillas
2	large egg yolks			Vegetable shortening, for frying
½	cup sugar			Melted butter (optional)
2	tablespoons all-purpose flour			Confectioners' sugar
½	cup (1 stick) butter or margarine			

Combine the pineapple, egg yolks, sugar, flour, and butter in a medium saucepan and cook over medium heat, stirring constantly, until the mixture thickens. Remove from the heat and set aside to cool. Spoon equal portions of the cooled pineapple mixture along the center of the tortillas. Roll up the tortillas and use wooden toothpicks to hold them together.

Heat the vegetable shortening in a large skillet until melted and hot, and fry the rollups until lightly browned on both sides. Remove them from the skillet and roll them in the melted butter, if desired, then in the confectioners' sugar.

Cook's Note: Canned pie filling can replace the pineapple mixture.

CINDY BROWN BROOKS
Greenville, Texas

Scatter Chunky Monkey Parfaits

Yield: 4 parfaits

Named for Elvis's beloved chimpanzee, Scatter, this peanut butter and banana dessert is a winner.

1	**(4-ounce) package instant chocolate pudding**
8	**plus 2 Nutter Butter cookies**
1	**ripe medium-size banana, sliced**

➤ Prepare the pudding with milk according to the package directions; refrigerate.

➤ Crush 8 cookies into crumbs on a large piece of wax paper. Spoon 1 tablespoon of the cookie crumbs into each of four, 4-ounce parfait glasses. Using half the pudding, divide it evenly among the glasses.

➤ Divide the sliced banana evenly among the four glasses. Add 1 tablespoon crushed cookies over the banana and top with the remaining pudding. Break the remaining 2 cookies in half, and stand a piece in each parfait as a garnish.

SHERRI STAGER
Mansfield, Pennsylvania
We Remember Elvis Fan Club of Pittsburgh

The Wonder of Your Crêpes

Yield: 12 servings

I was born in the north of Spain in an area called Asturias. During Carnival everyone enjoys frisuelos or crêpes, which are typical of the region and the village people there. After a wonderful visit to Graceland, I decided these delicious treats would have been worthy of Elvis's table.

1½	**cups all-purpose flour**
	Grated zest of 1 lemon
4	**large eggs, well beaten**
2	**cups milk**
1	**teaspoon vegetable oil**
2	**tablespoons sugar**
	Apple marmalade
	Vanilla ice cream
	Sliced fresh strawberries, for garnish

➤ Combine the flour, lemon zest, eggs, and milk in a medium bowl and mix well. Heat the oil in a small skillet. Add 1 or 2 tablespoons of the batter and move the pan around so that the batter covers the bottom. When the batter bubbles, turn it quickly to brown the other side.

➤ Remove the crêpe from the pan and set aside while you continue cooking, using up all the batter. Dust the crêpes with the sugar and serve them hot, rolled up with apple marmalade in the middle and ice cream on top. Garnish with the strawberries.

MARIA ALONSO-VEGAS FERNANDEZ
Madrid, Spain

"Mess of Blues" Pecan Bars

Yield: 12 to 15 bars

These bars rock—just like the King.

1¼	**cups all-purpose flour**
½	**cup (1 stick) butter, softened**
3	**tablespoons sugar**
¼	**teaspoon salt**
3	**to 4 tablespoons heavy cream**

PECAN TOPPING

¾	**cup (1½ sticks) butter**
¼	**cup light corn syrup**
3	**tablespoons heavy cream**
1	**cup packed light brown sugar**
2½	**teaspoons vanilla extract**
3	**cups toasted pecans**

➤ Preheat the oven to 350 degrees.

➤ Combine the flour, butter, sugar, and salt in a medium bowl. Add enough heavy cream to allow you to work the dough with your fingertips or a pastry cutter until coarse crumbs form. Press the crumbs into a 9 x13-inch baking pan. Bake 18 to 20 minutes or until lightly browned.

➤ While the bars are cooking make the topping. Combine the butter, corn syrup, cream, and brown sugar in a medium saucepan. Cook over medium heat, stirring constantly until the mixture boils, about 4 minutes. Stir in the vanilla and the pecans; stir well.

➤ Allow the crust to cool. Add the pecan topping and bake for 20 to 25 minutes longer. Allow the mixture to cool before cutting into bars.

SHERRY PATTERSON
Flower Mound, Texas

"A Little Less Conversation" Bars

Yield: 15 to 18 bars

Once you have one of these treats, you will want to talk less and eat more.

10	to 12 graham cracker squares
2	teaspoons dry vanilla pudding mix (not instant)
1	teaspoon unflavored gelatin
¼	cup plus 2 teaspoons milk
¼	cup (½ stick) butter or margarine, softened
1¼	cups dry roasted peanuts (about 12 ounces)
1	cup confectioners' sugar
25	caramel candies
1½	cups milk chocolate morsels

➤ Lightly grease the bottom and sides of a 9 x 9-inch baking dish. Place the graham crackers on the bottom. Fill in any cracks with broken crackers.

➤ Combine the pudding mix, gelatin, and ¼ cup milk in a 1-quart glass bowl; mix well. Let stand 5 minutes. Stir in the butter or margarine. Microwave on high for 2 to 3 minutes or until the mixture comes to a boil and thickens, stirring twice.

➤ Place the peanuts in a food processor; grind finely. Add ¼ cup of the peanuts to the pudding mixture; blend in the confectioners' sugar (the mixture will be very thick). Spoon the mixture onto the graham cracker base. Spread evenly and refrigerate for about 30 minutes or until set.

➤ Combine the caramels and 1 teaspoon of the remaining milk in a glass mixing bowl. Microwave on high for 2 to 2½ minutes or until soft, stirring at least once. Stir the mixture until smooth. Stir in the remaining ground peanuts (the mixture will be thick, so add drops of water if necessary). Spoon the caramel mixture evenly onto the refrigerated base.

➤ Combine the remaining 1 teaspoon milk with the milk chocolate morsels in a microwave-safe bowl. Microwave for 15 seconds; stir well. Microwave for 30 seconds; stir well. Continue to microwave on low until the chocolate mixture is smooth and spreadable (watch carefully so the mixture does not scorch; add another splash of milk if needed to make it spreadable).

➤ Pour over the caramel layer and refrigerate until set. Cut into squares to serve.

BECKE AMMONS
Fort Wayne, Indiana
Official Elvis Insider

Did You Know?

Elvis made history in 1997 by being the first performer to headline a live concert when he was no longer living. He performed in Memphis via video at a commemoration of the twentieth anniversary of his death.

"Merry Christmas, Baby" Berry Bars

Yield: 2 dozen bars

Elvis loved Christmas at Graceland. These berry treats would have been a welcome addition to his table.

2	**cups all-purpose flour**
1½	**cups regular oats**
¾	**cup plus 1 tablespoon firmly packed brown sugar**
1	**cup (2 sticks) butter or margarine, softened**
1	**(8-ounce) package cream cheese, softened**
1	**(14-ounce) can sweetened condensed milk**
¼	**cup bottled lemon juice**
2	**(16-ounce) cans whole berry cranberry sauce**
2	**tablespoons cornstarch**

➤ Preheat the oven to 350 degrees. Grease a 9 x 13-inch baking pan.

➤ Mix the flour, oats, ¾ cup brown sugar, and the butter in a large bowl with an electric mixer until crumbly. Set aside 1½ cups of the oat mix and press the remaining mix into the prepared pan. Bake for 15 minutes or until lightly browned.

➤ Beat the cream cheese in a medium bowl until fluffy. Beat in the milk until the mixture is smooth. Stir in the lemon juice. Spread over the baked crust. Combine the cranberry sauce, cornstarch, and the remaining 1 tablespoon of brown sugar in a small bowl. Spoon the mixture over the cream cheese layer. Top with the reserved crumb mixture.

➤ Bake for 45 minutes or until golden brown. Cool on a wire rack. Cut into bars to serve.

Cook's Note: Put a dollop of Triple Sec-flavored whipped cream on each serving, if you wish.

JAN FRANSEN
Bellingham, Washington

"It's Now or Never" Brownies with Fudge Topping

Yield: 10 to 12

2	**cups sugar**
1	**cup (2 sticks) butter or margarine**
1½	**cups all-purpose flour**
½	**teaspoon baking powder**
½	**teaspoon salt**
4	**tablespoons unsweetened cocoa powder**
4	**large eggs**
2	**teaspoons vanilla extract**

FUDGE TOPPING

1½	**cups confectioners' sugar**
2	**to 3 tablespoons unsweetened cocoa powder**
2	**tablespoons butter or margarine, softened**
1	**tablespoon vanilla extract**
2	**teaspoons milk, or more or less as needed**

➤ Preheat the oven to 350 degrees. Grease a 12 x 10-inch baking pan.

➤ Cream the sugar and butter together in a large bowl. Blend the flour, baking powder, salt, and cocoa powder in a medium bowl. Stir into the sugar mixture and blend well. Add the eggs and vanilla, mixing well.

➤ Pour the batter into the prepared baking pan and bake for 25 minutes or until a toothpick inserted in the center comes out clean.

➤ While the brownies are baking, make the topping. Combine the confectioners' sugar, cocoa, butter, and vanilla. Stir in just enough milk to make a mixture that is smooth and of spreading consistency. Remove the baking pan from the oven and spread the fudge topping on top of the brownies. Allow to cool before serving.

BRENDA SUE PICKLE
Bristow, Oklahoma
Simply Elvis Club

Old-Fashioned Sugar Cookies

Yield: about 2½ dozen cookies

1	cup sugar
½	cup (1 stick) butter, melted
2	large eggs
2½	cups all-purpose flour, or more as needed
2	teaspoons baking powder
¼	teaspoon salt
1	tablespoon milk or cream
1	teaspoon vanilla extract
	Sugar, for sprinkling (optional)
	Decorative sprinkles (optional)

CONFECTIONERS' SUGAR FROSTING

2	cups confectioners' sugar, or more as needed
1	tablespoon butter
2	tablespoons milk
1	teaspoon vanilla extract

➤ Preheat the oven to 425 degrees. Grease two cookie sheets.

➤ Combine the sugar and melted butter in a large bowl and mix well. Mix in the eggs. Combine the flour, baking powder, and salt in a medium bowl. Stir into the sugar mixture. Add the milk and vanilla and mix well. If the dough seems too wet, add a little more flour.

➤ Divide the dough into three portions. Roll out each portion on a floured surface to about ⅛ inch thick. Sprinkle with sugar or decorative sprinkles, if you wish, and cut with a cookie cutter.

➤ Bake the cookies for about 10 minutes.

➤ While the cookies are baking, make the frosting. Combine the sugar, butter, milk, and vanilla and mix well. If the mixture is too thin, add more confectioners' sugar. When the cookies are done, cool them on wire racks before frosting.

CARLENE ELVIK
Garden City, South Dakota
Official Elvis Insider

Texas Cow Patties

Yield: 4 dozen large cookies

2   cups (4 sticks) butter or margarine, softened
2   cups granulated sugar
2   cups firmly packed light brown sugar
4   large eggs
2   teaspoons vanilla extract
2   cups quick-cooking oats
2   cups cornflakes
4   cups all-purpose flour
2   teaspoons baking powder
2   teaspoons baking soda
1   (6-ounce) package semisweet chocolate morsels
2   cups chopped pecans

Preheat the oven to 325 degrees. Grease two cookie sheets.

Cream the butter and sugars together in a large bowl until light and fluffy. Add the eggs, one at a time, beating well after each addition. Stir in the vanilla. Add the oats and cornflakes, mixing thoroughly.

Stir together the flour, baking powder, and baking soda in a medium bowl. Gradually stir the flour mixture into the creamed mixture. Stir in the chocolate morsels and pecans. Drop by rounded tablespoonfuls onto the prepared cookie sheets.

Bake for 17 minutes; cool on a wire rack.

NAOMI NICHOLSON
Davie, Florida
Official Elvis Insider

Hunka Hunka Chocolate Chip Macadamia Cookies

Yield: about 3 dozen cookies

With the addition of the macadamia nuts, these cookies remind me of Elvis in Hawaii.

2¼	cups all-purpose flour
1	teaspoon salt
1	teaspoon baking soda
½	cup (1 stick) butter
½	cup vegetable shortening
¾	cup granulated sugar
¾	cup firmly packed light brown sugar
1	teaspoon vanilla extract
2	large eggs
1	(12-ounce) package chocolate chips
½	cup chopped walnuts
½	cup macadamia nuts

➤ Preheat the oven to 375 degrees. Line two cookie sheets with parchment paper.

➤ Combine the flour, salt, and baking soda in a large bowl.

➤ In a second large bowl, beat the butter, shortening, sugars, and vanilla with an electric mixer until creamy. Add the eggs one at a time, beating for 2 minutes after each addition. Slowly add the flour mixture to the moist ingredients; mix well and scrape the bottom of the bowl between additions. Add the chocolate chips and mix for 1 minute. Add the nuts and mix for 2 minutes.

➤ Using a medium-size ice-cream scoop, scoop the cookies onto the lined cookie sheets about 2 inches apart. Bake for about 10 minutes or until lightly browned. Cool on a rack until firm.

JUDITH MCELWAINE
Port Charlotte, Florida
The Elvis Lovers of South Gulf Cove

"Promised Land" Cookies

Yield: 2 to 2½ dozen cookies

I like to invent new cookie recipes. The day I made this one, I loaded the CD player with music and headed to the kitchen. Nothing came to me until "Burning Love" began to play. This recipe was inspired by Elvis's music and made with love.

1¾	**cups all-purpose flour**
¾	**teaspoon baking soda**
	Pinch of salt
1	**cup firmly packed dark brown sugar**
¼	**cup unsweetened cocoa powder**
2	**teaspoons ground chocolate**
¾	**cup (1½ sticks) butter or margarine, softened**
1	**large egg**
1	**teaspoon vanilla extract**
6	**to 8 ounces semisweet chocolate pieces**
1	**cup chopped pecans**

➤ Preheat the oven to 375 degrees.

➤ Sift the flour, baking soda, and salt in a large bowl. Add the brown sugar, cocoa, and ground chocolate. Mix well with a wooden spoon. Add the butter, egg, and vanilla. Mix the batter well, until no lumps of flour remain. Then add the chocolate pieces and pecans and mix well. With a spoon, drop the cookie dough onto a cookie sheet about 1 to 2 inches apart.

➤ Bake for 10 to 12 minutes. Remove the cookies to wire racks to cool.

LORI YEASAYER
Atlanta, Georgia

"If I Can Dream" Heavenly Cookies

Yield: 1½ dozen cookies

2¼	**cups quick-cooking oats**
1½	**cups all-purpose flour**
¼	**teaspoon salt**
1	**teaspoon baking powder**
1	**teaspoon baking soda**
½	**cup (1 stick) butter**
1½	**cups peanut butter**
½	**cup granulated sugar**
1	**cup packed light brown sugar**
3	**egg whites**
1½	**teaspoons vanilla extract**
2	**cups miniature marshmallows**
⅓	**cup chocolate chips**
1½	**cups chocolate-covered pretzels, crushed**

➤ Preheat the oven to 350 degrees. Lightly grease a 9 x 13-inch baking pan.

➤ Combine the oats, flour, salt, baking powder, and baking soda in a medium bowl; mix well. Combine the butter and peanut butter in a large bowl and mix until smooth. Add the sugars, egg whites, and vanilla; mix well. Stir the oat mixture into the butter mixture; mix well.

➤ Spoon the mixture into the prepared baking pan. Cover with the marshmallows and chocolate chips.

➤ Bake for 18 to 20 minutes or until the marshmallows puff on top. Remove from the oven and spread the pretzels over the top, pressing down lightly to make sure they stick. Cool well before cutting.

Cook's Note: Use a wet knife to cut the cookies.

REBECCA CRAWFORD-SHURTZ
Berkley, Michigan

"Heartbreak Hotel®" Peanut Butter Drops

Yield: 15 cookies

1	cup sugar
1	cup smooth peanut butter
1	large egg
15	chocolate kisses

- ➤ Preheat the oven to 325 degrees.

- ➤ Combine the sugar, peanut butter, and egg in a medium bowl. Drop by heaping teaspoonfuls onto an ungreased cookie sheet. Place an unwrapped chocolate kiss in the middle of each ball of dough.

- ➤ Bake for 8 to 10 minutes.

Cook's Note: These cookies spread when baking, so leave some room between each ball of dough.

PATRICIA ATKINS
Bourbon, Missouri
Official Elvis Insider

It Was a Very Great Time in My Life

I never quit my job at Baptist Hospital, and I never took a salary from Elvis Presley. He got sick in '75 and Dr. Nick [George Nickopoulus] came up to my floor—I was the unit supervisor—and told me he was coming into the hospital and that he wanted me to take care of him. He then told me that he'd let me know when Elvis was coming in—they had to talk him into it—and I said okay. He called me one afternoon and said Elvis was coming in early the next morning and he'd like me to be with him. So I said, 'Tomorrow is my day off,' and he said, 'Oh come on, Miz Cocke, won't you do this? This guy is a really shy guy and he would feel so much better if he had you with him.'

"So I said okay. Well, he called me at about 4 o'clock the next morning and said Elvis was coming in. I showered and dressed and went in. It's funny, I'd never been one of his followers—he was just out of my range. In fact, I was offered front row tickets to a concert one time and I turned them down. Dr. Nick knew me, and he knew that I was older, and I guess he thought that I wasn't going to go gaga over a celebrity. And then when I turned him down, I think he really knew he'd made the right choice.

"But when I went into the building that morning, I knew the minute I walked in the door that Elvis was already there. There was a static electricity in the air that was just overpowering. That might sound funny, but it's the truth. I got off at the floor and started walking down the hall, and the next thing I knew I was flying on a cloud down the hall. I was so excited to meet this guy. And I hadn't even wanted to go.

"When I got to the room, Linda Thompson was shaving him. Joe Esposito was also in the room along with Al Strata and a couple of other people, and Dr. Nick.

"Dr. Nick introduced me to Linda and said, 'You know who this is,' and he grinned at me and I grinned at him. And almost immediately Joe got up and said, 'Well it's time for us to go. We'll see you later.' Then he came back in the room and said, 'Listen, Boss, we need to talk about getting some private-duty nurses for you.' Elvis said, 'Well, I want to talk to Miz Cocke first, and then I'll decide what I want to do about private duty nurses.'

"So we spent the whole day together, and at about one or one-thirty he asked me what I wanted him to do about private duty nurses. He said, 'I'll have them if you want me to, but I want you to be the one who takes care of me.' And I said, 'Well, Honey, if you have me, you don't need private duty nurses.' So he never ever had private duty nurses. I took care of him during the day and had the charge nurses take care of him in the evening and overnight.

"He was in the hospital three weeks that time. He left and came back—I was going home one day in August when Dr. Nick told me he was coming back, and he wanted the same suite he'd had before. There was a man in the room; but when we explained the problem, he agreed to move and we got him another suite. I went on at nine and stayed with him all night. It then got to the point where he wanted me to stay in the hospital all night even though I had someone else assigned to take care of him. So he got me a room right next to his. Then when he went home, he needed someone to monitor his blood pressure; and he asked me if I would come and sleep at Graceland. I told him I couldn't do that. I had a job and I had a family. He asked me if I'd talk to my family. And in the end, I'd work my shift, then go home and shower, have dinner with my family, and then I'd go to Graceland to sleep. That was supposed to be for two weeks but it wound up being two and a half years on and off. Sometimes I'd go out there in the daytime and visit with his Aunt Delta and his grandmother. Sometimes I'd stay the night, and sometimes I'd just go and give him a good back rub.

"He was a nice young man and I was very fond of him. It was a very great time in my life. We never talked about his being Elvis Presley, the King of Rock and Roll—in fact he never wanted anyone to call him that. He said there's only one king and that's Christ. We didn't talk about his career or the places he'd been. We talked about family things. We usually sat in Lisa's room at night and watched television—there was a day bed in there and he brought in a big chair—and he'd eat his meals there and then he'd go back to his room and go to bed.

"It was a real different time in my life. Just a couple of days before he died, he called me at about two o'clock in the morning and asked me to come out and be with him. So I went out there and I sat with him and held his hand until about 6:30 in the morning, when he said, 'I think I can go to sleep now.' So I told him I'd check back with him later and I left. That was the last time I spoke to him face to face. On the morning he died, he called and asked me to come give him a back rub because he was very tired and he was leaving on tour. So I said I'd be out as soon as I got off work, and the next time I saw him was when he came into the hospital and he was DOA.

"Once he asked me if I knew how to make banana pudding; and I said, 'Sure I do.' So he asked me to bring him one. I said, 'But you have six cooks in this house. You want me to bring you banana pudding?' And he said, 'Yes, I want you to bring me a banana pudding.' So I said, 'Okay, I'll bring one out here tomorrow when I come.' And he said, 'Don't leave it downstairs because you brought two pies out here one day. You left them downstairs, and I never even got any.' So I said, 'Okay,' and I brought it up and put it in the little refrigerator that was in Lisa's room.

"The next day we were in there drinking our coffee, and he asked me if I'd brought the pudding. I said, 'Yes,' and he said, 'Where is it?' And I said, 'It's right here in the refrigerator.' So he asked me to bring it to him, and he took the bowl and a spoon and ate about half of it right out of the bowl; and then he went back the next night and finished it. [Marian Cocke's Banana Pudding recipe follows.]

"A lot of people have asked me what was the fondest memory I have of Elvis, and I've always said, 'Every moment.' But I guess if I had to really pick two special times, one would be the time he reached over and put his hand on my knee and said, 'You know, Miz Cocke, you're one of the few people who's never asked one thing of me.'

"And then one Christmas time he gave me a really beautiful ring. I had it on one night, and we had gone for a ride. We were going up the driveway, and we were both sitting in the back seat. He reached over and picked up my hand and said, 'Who gave you that ring?' And I said, 'Oh, a rich old boyfriend.' And he picked up my hand and kissed it and said, 'Does this ring tell you how that rich old boyfriend feels about you?'

"If I ever had anything to say about Elvis Presley, it would be that he cared more about other people than he did about himself. He really genuinely cared about other people.

"I think that Elvis really cared about me and what happened to me, as I did about him. I was always protective of him during the time I was with him, and I still am. He was very, very decent to me. He was very polite, and he never called me by my first name. Therefore, no one else in the house did either, except his Aunt Delta and his grandma. George Klein still won't call me by my first name. It was a very different time. He was a nice man; he truly was."

MARIAN COCKE,
Memphis, Tennessee

Marian Cocke's Banana Pudding

Yield: 4 servings (unless you're Elvis)

1	**cup sugar**
¼	**cup all-purpose flour**
	Dash of salt
1½	**cups half-and-half**
1½	**cups milk**
3	**egg yolks**
3	**tablespoons butter**
	Vanilla extract
	Vanilla wafers
	Sliced bananas
	Whipped cream or whipped topping

➤ In a bowl combine the sugar and flour. Mix in the salt, half-and-half, milk, and egg yolks. Transfer to a saucepan and cook, stirring, over medium heat until thickened.

➤ Remove from the heat and stir in the butter and vanilla to taste. Cool the custard to room temperature.

➤ Layer a glass bowl with the vanilla wafers and sliced bananas. Pour in the custard, top with another layer of wafers and bananas, cover with whipped cream or whipped topping, and refrigerate until ready to serve.

MARIAN COCKE
Memphis, Tennessee

"TCB" Ice Cream Delight

Yield: 2 servings

2	**tablespoons peanut butter**
2	**flour tortillas**
2	**ripe bananas**
1	**cup canola oil**
2	**scoops vanilla ice cream**
2	**tablespoons cinnamon**
2	**tablespoons chocolate sauce**
2	**tablespoons honey**
2	**teaspoons confectioners' sugar**

Spread the peanut butter evenly on the tortillas. Roll a banana in each tortilla and seal the roll with a dab of peanut butter. Heat the oil in a large skillet and pan-fry the wrapped bananas over medium heat until slightly golden. Drain on paper towels and set aside to cool.

Place the wrapped bananas in the oven for a few minutes to reheat. Scoop the ice cream into two banana split dishes. Cut the tortillas in half and place a half on either side of the ball of ice cream. Sprinkle with the cinnamon, drizzle with the chocolate sauce and honey, and then sprinkle with the confectioners' sugar. Serve immediately.

TRAVIS REDMON
Knoxville, Tennessee
The Pizza Kitchen

"Double Trouble" Trifle

Yield: 6 to 8 servings

1	sponge cake or 1 package ladyfingers
1	(28-ounce) can fruit cocktail
½	cup sherry (or brandy)

HOMEMADE CUSTARD

½	cup sugar
⅓	cup all-purpose flour
	Dash of salt
4	large egg yolks
2	cups milk
½	teaspoon vanilla extract
1	ripe banana
2	cups freshly whipped cream
	Shaved chocolate or sprinkles, for topping

➤ Tear the sponge cake into small pieces; place the pieces of sponge cake, or the ladyfingers in the bottom of a deep, glass dish. Drain the fruit cocktail, reserving 2 tablespoons of the juice, and spoon the fruit over the cake. Combine the sherry and the 2 tablespoons of fruit cocktail juice, and pour the mixture over the fruit. Cover and let soak for 1 hour or overnight.

➤ Prepare the custard. Combine the sugar, flour, and salt in the top of a double boiler. Stir in the egg yolks and milk and blend well. Cook, uncovered, over boiling water, stirring constantly, until the mixture is thickened, about 5 minutes. Remove from the heat and stir in the vanilla. Cool before adding the custard to the trifle.

➤ Pour the cooled custard over the fruit and chill. Just before serving, slice the banana over the custard, top with the whipped cream, and decorate with the chocolate shavings or sprinkles.

KAREN ALDERSON
Calgary, Alberta, Canada
Founding member, Official Elvis Insider
Elvis Presley Fan Club of Great Britain

FROM ELVIS'S KITCHEN

Banana Pudding

Yield: 4 to 6 servings

6	cups milk	½	cup (1 stick) butter
8	large eggs, separated	2	tablespoons vanilla extract
2½	cups plus 1 tablespoon sugar	1	large box vanilla wafers
3	tablespoons cornstarch	4	ripe bananas, sliced

➤ Preheat the oven to 350 degrees.

➤ Mix the milk, egg yolks, 2½ cups sugar, the cornstarch, and butter in a medium saucepan and bring to a boil; boil slowly, stirring constantly, until thick. Stir in the vanilla.

➤ Layer the vanilla wafers in a 9 x 13-inch baking pan. Top with the sliced bananas. Pour the hot milk mixture over the bananas and wafers.

➤ Beat the egg whites in a medium bowl. Add the remaining 1 tablespoon sugar and beat until stiff peaks form. Spoon the egg whites over the top of the pudding.

➤ Bake the pudding for about 10 minutes or until the topping is lightly browned.

Blue Hawaiian Pineapple

Yield: 4 to 6 servings

¾	cup sugar	¼	cup milk
2	large eggs	2	(8-ounce) cans crushed pineapple, drained
¼	cup (½ stick) butter or margarine, softened	2	cups soft bread cubes

➤ Preheat the oven to 350 degrees. Grease a 2-quart casserole dish.

➤ Combine the sugar, eggs, butter, and milk in a large bowl and mix well. Stir in the pineapple and bread cubes. Pour into the prepared baking dish and bake, covered, for 1 hour. Serve warm.

BOBBI J. TURNER
Waynesboro, Pennsylvania
President, Elvis Memories Fan Club

Bossa Nova
Bread-and-Butter Pudding

Yield: 5 servings

I would have loved for Elvis to try this recipe. He would have liked the sweet, creamy texture of the hot pudding.

2	**cups milk**
2	**large eggs, lightly beaten**
½	**cup sugar**
1	**teaspoon ground cinnamon**
¼	**teaspoon salt**
6	**to 8 slices lightly buttered white bread, crusts removed**
½	**cup raisins**

➤ Combine the milk, eggs, sugar, cinnamon, and salt in a large bowl; beat lightly. Grease a 1½-quart glass casserole dish with butter. Cut the bread slices in half. Layer half the bread in the dish and sprinkle it with half the raisins; lay the remaining bread slices over the top and sprinkle with the remaining raisins. Pour the milk mixture over the bread and soak for 10 minutes.

➤ Place the baking dish in the microwave oven, and cook on 5 or medium for 26 to 28 minutes. Let stand for 5 minutes before serving.

KAREN ALDERSON
Calgary, Alberta, Canada
Founding Member, Official Elvis Insider
Elvis Presley Fan Club of Great Britain

"Loving You"
Pecan-Raisin Bread Pudding

Yield: 6 to 8 servings

This is comfort food like Mama used to make.

1	**(1-pound) loaf cinnamon swirl bread**
3	**cups milk**
4	**large eggs**
1	**tablespoon vanilla extract**
¾	**cup sugar**
½	**teaspoon ground cinnamon**
¼	**teaspoon nutmeg**
¼	**cup raisins soaked in 2 ounces hazelnut syrup**
¼	**cup pecans or pecan pieces**
	Additional hazelnut syrup (optional)

HAZELNUT SAUCE

6	**tablespoons butter**
1	**cup sugar**
½	**cup condensed milk**
2	**tablespoons hazelnut syrup**
1	**tablespoon vanilla extract**

➤ Cut the bread into cubes and place the cubes in a large bowl. Combine the milk, eggs, vanilla, sugar, cinnamon, and nutmeg in a medium bowl. Add the milk mixture to the bread cubes. Add the drained, plumped raisins and the pecans. Add more hazelnut syrup, if desired. Toss lightly and let sit for 15 minutes.

➤ Preheat the oven to 350 degrees. Grease a 9 x 13-inch baking dish.

➤ Spoon the bread mixture into the prepared pan and bake for 30 to 35 minutes or until crispy brown.

➤ While the pudding is baking, prepare the sauce. Melt the butter in a small saucepan and add the sugar, condensed milk, syrup, and vanilla. Bring to a boil for 1 minute, stirring constantly. Serve the pudding with warm Hazelnut Sauce.

CHEF JOHN RUMNEY, CDM, CFPP
Grant, Michigan

"Tutti Frutti" Raspberry Divinity

Yield: 24 to 36 pieces

This would make a great addition to the Christmas treats at Graceland. It melts in your mouth.

3	cups sugar
¾	cup corn syrup
½	cup hot water
2	large egg whites
1	(3-ounce) package raspberry gelatin
1	cup chopped nuts of your choice

➤ Cook the sugar, syrup, and water in a medium saucepan over medium-high heat, stirring often, until the mixture reaches the hard-ball stage. Beat the egg whites until foamy; then add the gelatin and beat until the whites form stiff peaks. Slowly beat in the hot syrup and continue beating until a spoonful of the mixture will hold its shape. Stir in the nuts.

➤ Using an ice cream scoop dipped in water, spoon the fudge onto wax paper. When it has cooled, store in an airtight container with wax paper between the layers. It can also be frozen in the container, if you wish.

CATHY WAGGONER
Webb City, Missouri
Return to Sender Club

Peanut Butter and Nanner Goo Balls

Yield: 12 to 15 balls

1 cup light corn syrup	5 cups cornflakes
1 cup sugar	1 to 2 ripe medium bananas, sliced
1½ cups smooth peanut butter	

➤ In a medium saucepan bring the syrup and sugar just to a boil over medium heat.

➤ Remove from the heat and stir in the peanut butter until smooth. Pour in the cornflakes and bananas; stir well. Drop the mixture by tablespoonfuls onto wax paper to set.

ROSE ROCKWELL
Logan, Utah

Peanut Butter Fudge

Yield: 32 small squares

2 cups sugar	4 tablespoons smooth peanut butter
¾ cup milk	
Pinch of baking soda	½ teaspoon vanilla extract
3 tablespoons light corn syrup	

➤ Combine the sugar, milk, baking soda, and corn syrup in a medium saucepan. Bring to a boil over medium heat, stirring well. (Test by dropping small amounts of the mixture into a glass of cold water; it's ready when it forms a small ball or registers 234 degrees on a candy thermometer.)

➤ Add the peanut butter and vanilla; stir well with a wooden spoon until thickened. Pour into a well-greased, 9 x 9-inch, glass dish. Cool, and then cut into small squares to serve.

STANLEY A. GUERIN
Belleville, Michigan

"Crying in the Chapel" Stained Glass Windows

Yield: 36 pieces

This is a family favorite at Christmas or any time.

1	**(16-ounce) package semisweet chocolate chips**
½	**cup (1 stick) butter or margarine**
1	**(16-ounce) package colored mini-marshmallows**
1	**cup chopped walnuts or pecans**

➤ Melt the chocolate chips and butter in the top of a double-broiler over low heat, stirring often. Stir in the marshmallows and nuts. Let the marshmallows melt slightly; then pour portions of the mixture onto sheets of parchment paper.

➤ Form into rolls and refrigerate. Cut into small slices immediately before serving.

Cook's Note: You can sprinkle shredded coconut on the parchment paper before adding the mixture, if desired.

VICKY MITCHELL
Houston, Texas

Elvis touching his fans forever.

Index

Boldface page numbers refer to photo insert